To Tom —

Thanks for making [...] that help keep the Spirit of the [...] alive and well in America !

RICK HACKER
his mark

THE
MUZZLELOADING
HUNTER

THE
MUZZLELOADING
HUNTER

being a complete guide
for the black powder sportsman

BY

RICK HACKER

WINCHESTER PRESS
Tulsa, Oklahoma
1981

Library of Congress Cataloging in Publication Data

Hacker, Rick, 1942–
    The muzzleloading hunter.

    1. Hunting. 2. Muzzle-loading firearms.
I. Title.
SK39.2.H3   799.2'028'3   81-10509
ISBN 0-87691-354-0   AACR2

Published by Winchester Press
1421 South Sheridan Road
P. O. Box 1260
Tulsa, Oklahoma 74101

Book design by Quentin Fiore

Printed in the United States of America

1 2 3 4 5   85 84 83 82 81

To Joan
— this is the book I was telling you about.

PREFACE

It is common knowledge among most writers that few authors ever get rich writing a book. However, this only holds true if you measure your wealth by monetary standards, for in creating *The Muzzleloading Hunter*, I have found a treasure that is invaluable by all other measures: the privilege of updating one of the most classic of my literary loves, the black powder sportsman's handbook. Most of these popular works were written from the 1850's until the 1880's, and many are rare collectibles today. Of course, they all dealt with the nineteenth-century outdoorsman. To my knowledge, *The Muzzleloading Hunter* is the first hardcover treatise on this time-honored sport to be written in recent history for the twentieth-century outdoorsman. As such, I have tried to make it as complete and comprehensive as possible, drawing not only from my own hunting and black powder experiences, but from the knowledge of others as well. And therein lies my second source of wealth: the numerous friends I have made over the years as a result of my interest and writings in muzzleloading and hunting, priceless people within the shooting industry as well as individuals who follow other vocations and just like to shoot black powder.

Of course, no endeavor such as this can ever be a one-man job, and it is a gross understatement to say that without the faith, friendship, and follow-through of numerous individuals, you would not be reading this book now, for it would not exist. Most of these individuals or their companies are mentioned during our journey through the pages ahead. However, there are others, those people who have elected to work behind the scenes and whose identity is rarely made public. Directly or indirectly, they have played a notable role in whatever success this book may enjoy. Yet, to try and name them all only invites the possibility of omitting some of the people you want to remember most. For example, if I began by mentioning two of the muzzleloading industry's most efficient and reliable coordinators, Sharon Cunningham and Becky Atkins, then I might forget Penny Kappler and her two Jean-Claudes. Of course, my amigo Phil Spangenberger should definitely be riding in this column. But what if I forgot Lee Fry? And how about John Heshion and Tom Sheppard? Do I mention them too? Surely I must, just as I would have to mention another hardworking twosome, Merilee and Leonard Allen. Then there's the risk of omitting Carol Tuschick; she might be forgiving, but I am not so sure about Phil Chase, even though he has a beard. But what about Paul Beck?

If I gave a single-shot salute to John Schoffstall and Wolf Droege, what about Ron Mosier and Rex Thomas? Of course, I could never forgive myself if I forgot to include kindred spirit Garry James, B. F. (before flintlocks). I could go on, but I think I would be inviting danger, so I just don't think I'll mention anyone, including those named above. But I do want to publicly acknowledge Petersen Publications and *Guns & Ammo* for their unselfish support in permitting me to use photographs and portions of text from some of my articles that have appeared in their publications.

There is one individual who deserves an entire paragraph to herself, and that is my wife, Joan. Although she is not a hunter and has only fired a percussion rifle a few times in her life, she has more pioneer spirit than most men. Without ever asking, she just naturally helped assume the workload of this book, unselfishly devoting seven days a week in translating my handwritten notes and smoothly typing my final copy so that a civilized person could read it without the use of a mirror. Whenever I screamed and raged about certain products that had failed to live up to expectations, she stood by, ready with words of consolation. Yet through it all, there was never a complaint; the only murmur of dissent I ever heard was the occasional lament, "I wish just once we could eat dinner before eight o'clock," as she waited while I, lashed to my typewriter with rawhide, pounded out the pages you now hold in your hand. Quite literally, this book has been a labor of love.

I also owe a great debt of gratitude to my publisher, specifically Editor-in-Chief Bob Elman and his production sidekick Joy Flora, whose combined faith in *The Muzzleloading Hunter* rivals my own, and was the inspiration that led to the graphic treatment that has made this book appear as if it just came out of the nineteenth century, even though it is written for the modern day black powder hunter. The basic design for the page layouts was styled after books our forefathers read. The line illustrations that set the theme for each chapter date from the 1840's to the 1860's and were taken from some of the original nineteenth-century hunting books in my personal collection. Thus, this book is as close a link with the past as the very muzzleloaders we hunt with.

In selecting the various products for this book, my main criterion was quality: does the product work, is it well-made, and is it a good value for the money. This latter concern is especially important, for, due to our ever-changing economy, no prices are given as they would probably go out-of-date even as you are reading this. Of course, I suspect there are some firms whose dedicated work has escaped detection, and you are encouraged to seek these people out by exploring the various ads which fill the pages of the publications listed in Chapter Ten. Still, in an effort to make *The Muzzleloading Hunter* as comprehensive as possible, I have discovered that the companies covered in this book are as diverse as the individuals participating in our sport, and range from one-man operations to multimillion-dollar corporations.

The name, address and a brief description (when needed) of every company mentioned in this book will be found listed alphabetically under "Outfitters & Suppliers" in Chapter Ten. Thus, when you come across a company whose product interests you and you want to contact them (although many firms sell through retail sporting goods outlets only), just flip to the last chapter. In addition, some firms known by more than one name are cross-referenced (i.e., Uncle Mike's — see Michael's of Oregon). You should be able to find everything you need using just this book.

In reading a chapter from George Frederick Ruxton's *Adventures in Mexico and The Rocky Mountains*, first published in 1848, I came across an interesting description of the Far West trappers and hunters of those days:

> ... Knowing no wants save those of nature, their sole care is to provide sufficient food to support life, and the necessary clothing to protect them from rigorous climate. This, with the assistance of their trusty rifles, they are generally able to effect, but sometimes at the expense of great peril and hardship ... The costume of the trapper is a hunting shirt of dressed buckskins

... and pantaloons of the same material. A flexible felt hat and moccasins clothe his extremities. Over his left shoulder and under his right arm hang his powder horn and bullet pouch, in which he carries his balls, flint and steel and odds and ends of all kinds. Round the waist is a belt in which is stuck a huge butcher knife in a sheath of buffalo hide ... a tomahawk is also added; and of course, a long, heavy rifle is part and parcel of his equipment.

Aside from a few minor improvements (which are discussed later on in this book), I was immediately struck with the similarity between Ruxton's description of the hunter of the 1840's and the muzzleloading hunter of today. Are we emulating that long-ago image, or merely following a natural path that has always been there for those who want to take it? It really does not matter, for the sport of black powder hunting is as vast as the great outdoors, and provides plenty of room for all who wish to partake of it, be they primitive buckskinner, or advanced "modern," or someone in-between. Each style of hunter should be welcomed into the other's camp, in the true spirit of sharing a common bond, for no element of our sport is any greater than the other. Our combined participation is what makes it—and us—strong and able to endure.

When I first began hunting with a muzzleloader, there were no longer any old-timers who could pass on the hunting secrets of an earlier age. I had to learn from trial and error, and from reading of the way things used to be. We are in a different period of history now, a better one for us, and it is my hope that perhaps this book can be your "old-timer," to sit with, learn from, and enjoy.

May the Spirit of the Hunt always ride with you, and may both your shots and thoughts be true.

RICK HACKER

his mark

This 10th day of September 1981.

CONTENTS

THE
MUZZLELOADING
HUNTER

WEEDER—CHUBB

CHAPTER ONE

THE HUNTER'S HERITAGE

ince the dawn of his existence over three million years
ago, the species of man, like all carnivores, has been a
hunter — not so much by choice as by evolution and experience, which have caused him to acquire and refine the very elements necessary for his survival. Although a kin of other creatures
born of the wilderness, man soon found that what he lacked in
speed, sight, and hearing ability, he more than made up for with in-
tellect. It was man who learned to stand upright, thereby elevating
his line of vision so that he might see farther in all directions.
Through a fortunate blend of chance and curiosity, he eventually
discovered fire, and subsequently the ability to bend, shape, and
fashion metals into weapons that ensured his survival, both in terms
of defense as well as food gathering. The existence of gunpowder,
first made known to the Western world in the thirteenth century,
had surprisingly little initial effect upon man's hunting prowess. It
took 300 years for him to finally regard this new substance seriously
enough to fashion firearms for it, and then another two centuries for
those weapons to reach a state of design perfection that made them
both reliable and effective. That was when the age of the muzzleloading hunter was born. From the mid-1700's until the latter part of
the nineteenth century, well past the advent of metallic cartridges,
and even on into the smokeless powder era, the front-loading sportsman reached a state of prowess and expertise with his food-gather-

ing weapon that had never previously been known and whose effect is still felt today, perhaps with more meaning than ever before.

With his flintlock, the backwoodsman of the eastern shores learned marksmanship and stalking skills. Half a century later, armed with his big caliber heavy plains rifle, the hunter confirmed that there was no animal on the North American continent too large or too dangerous to be dropped with a properly-placed muzzleloading ball. Even when the fast-shooting repeating rifles, such as the Henry and Winchester lever-actions arrived on the sporting scene during the 1860's and 1870's, the muzzleloader was still retained by knowledgeable hunters, for they knew that the single-shot front-loading rifle was the only firearm whose time-tested design was strong enough to safely handle those bone-crushing charges necessary for effective big game hunting. Moreover, the smaller-bored patch and ball rifles usually outshot their metallic cartridge counterparts, a reputation that is still upheld today in many regional turkey shoots, where firing at a "mark" with open sights is a time-honored tradition.

For more than 150 years, the muzzleloading rifle and shotgun became the hunter's trustworthy ally. In his hands they provided food, procured skins for clothing and trade, and helped teach youngsters the necessary and universal fundamentals of sportsmanship, confidence, and pride, while perpetuating a national right of responsible gun ownership and use — a freedom that existed nowhere else in the world. But the muzzleloading hunting rifle was more than just a teacher and a tool; it was the key that opened up the vast reaches of the American frontier, and enabled early pathfinders to lay eyes on untouched forests and valleys and later upon the horizon-reaching expanse of the Great Plains and still later upon the lofty wonders of the Rockies, the Sierras, and finally the endless Pacific itself. It was the muzzleloaders and the men who carried them into the unknown, that first met with and dispelled danger in voluminous clouds of white smoke, taming an unpredictable land, and setting the stage for one of the greatest dramas known to modern history: the eventual expansion and settling of our country from ocean to ocean in less than 200 years. The cartridge-shooting Colts and Winchesters may have "won the

Forerunner of today's muzzleloading hunter. A gentleman hunter of the 1630's shoulders his 12-pound matchlock in preparation for firing. The .65 caliber smoothbore was ignited by a smoldering flaxen cord that had been soaked in vinegar or potassium nitrate. This system of ignition, crude as it seems, rarely resulted in misfires. Note the bandoleer of wooden "cartridges" hanging from the musketeer's belt, marking one of the earliest uses of premeasured charges.

West," but it was the muzzleloader that originally opened up the game and set the stakes!

Indeed, only after the introduction and eventual acceptance of harder-cast steels, and harder-hitting cartridges, did the muzzleloader finally lose ground to the smokeless powder hunting gun. But long after the thick black powder smoke dissipated in the winds of progress, a spark of remembrance and reverence still remained in the mind of the American sportsman. Even after the turn of the century, that glow was kept alive for over 50 years by a few die-hard shooters, men who refused to forget the guns of our country's past. Craftsmen like Royland Southgate and Hacker Martin kept those traditions alive by continuing to manufacture muzzleloaders with the same handcrafted skill of the nineteenth century, threading their own screws and hand-cutting the rifling one groove at a time.

And more than a few individualists (a suitably noble term for them) continued to hunt with their "old smokepoles," sometimes out of necessity — for muzzleloaders were inexpensive to shoot and often were all that was available — and sometimes out of love or just for the sheer thrill of it. Men like Ned Roberts and Sgt. Alvin York shot at game with patch and ball during a time when the bolt action rifle and the semiautomatic pistol were the norm.

Unfortunately, in times of crisis, history can be a fickle and disposable thing. And so it was during World War II and later, in the postwar construction boom, that the legacy of the muzzleloading hunter was temporarily lost, kept alive only by the dedicated activities of groups such as the National Muzzle Loading Rifle Association and periodic literary efforts of a few "old time" gun writers who found a forum for their knowledge and thoughts in an occasional sporting magazine article and a few books and reprints.

But then a curious phenomenon began taking shape in the outdoorsman's world: We began discovering our past. Originally in this country, the sport of muzzleloading hunting got its start in the East, later reaching its most romantic period in the opening of the North and the Far West. But the rebirth of the twentieth century black powder hunter was spawned in the South, through two unrelated events. First, a real-life Appalachian pathfinder named Davy Crockett was brought into the American limelight by Walt Disney Studios in the early 1950's. Due to a remarkable and far-reaching combination of books, music, movies, and a television series, the characterization of this legendary Tennessean with his long gun, buckskins and coonskin cap, was eagerly accepted, not only in America, but throughout the world, where he represented a refreshing alternative to the six-gun western, and no doubt, epitomized everything that straight-shooting, fearless, and honest America stood for. And for the first time, Americans realized that they had a picturesque history that pre-dated the cowboy...the era of the black powder hunter.

Turner Kirkland, America's twentieth century black powder pioneer, fulfilled one of his dreams by going to Africa on a muzzleloading safari. Here he is shown with a bull elephant he dropped with a shot from each barrel of his century-old Belgium 4-gauge double. He had purchased the gun years ago and had it refurbished in the hope of using it for just such an adventure.

About the same time the Crockett phenomenon was making its appearance, another Tennessean named Turner Kirkland was busy selling antique muzzleloading gun parts out of his father's garage in the tucked-away town of Union City, Tennessee. With all this interest in black powder shooting, he thought, wouldn't it be nice if someone made a replica muzzleloading rifle, as there were not enough originals to go around. And thus it was that Turner Kirkland, through his company Dixie Gun Works, became the first individual to mass-produce a replica muzzleloader. He called it the New Dixie Squirrel Rifle and the first 200 guns were spoken for before they were even completed. It is interesting to note that this pioneer replica was a *hunting* arm. Patterned after the Kentucky rifle, it was available in either flintlock or percussion, came in .40 caliber, rifled one turn in 48 inches, and was fitted with open sights which were to be drifted and filed "on target" by the shooter, just as the old timers used to do. Approximately 25,000 of Dixie's squirrel guns were made from 1957 to 1978; most of them are still in use and they are rarely encountered for sale on the used gun market. No longer available today (having been replaced by Dixie's Tennessee Mountain Rifle), the Squirrel Rifle is gradually gaining the status of a collector's arm as well as a hunting gun, having been acclaimed as the first replica front-loader, the one which started a trend.

Shortly after the Squirrel Gun's appearance, another black powder devotee, Val Forgett, decided to blend his manufacturing and technical expertise with his historical knowledge. In 1957, he established the Navy Arms Company. On the eve of our country's Civil War Centennial, Val's gun magazine ads, featuring a crossed pair of 1851-styled "Yank" and "Reb" pistols, stirred the interest of the shooting world. Later, Navy Arms went on to pioneer the use of investment castings in replica black powder pistols, as well as introducing the world's first stainless steel cap and ball revolver, an 1858 Remington Army.

With these two industry leaders in the forefront, the muzzleloading race was on. Oddly enough, no one knows exactly how many black powder shooters there are today, but it is safe to say they number in the hundreds of thousands worldwide and each year the sport of charcoal burning attracts thousands more to its ranks. The biggest concentration, of course, is in America, but according to

Val Forgett, the first man to begin mass producing replicas of pre-existing black powder arms was also the first to test his guns on the beasts of Africa.

mail order sources, the largest numbers of overseas shooters reside in England, Australia, and New Zealand.

Although reasons for purchasing a muzzleloader range from "historical curiosity" to plinking, ever since the mid-1970's, an interesting trend has been taking place: Firearms industry sources state that approximately 70 percent of all muzzleloaders are purchased for hunting — an impressive number considering the fact that there are over twenty million hunters in the United States, or roughly, one out of every eleven persons. Traditional hunting-styled weapons such as the Hawken and plainer-grade Kentucky Rifles have always been popular with shooters, but so strong is the sporting call today that there are entire new breeds of front-loaders, such as the Thompson/Center Renegade and Sile Hunter Carbine, that have been created strictly for game-getting rather than historical design (although it should be pointed out that eighteenth and nineteenth century-designed muzzleloaders are equally effective as hunting weapons; gun design is largely a matter of personal choice, as we shall discuss in the next chapter).

There are many reasons for the dominance of hunting as the primary lure that attracts shooters to the muzzleloading field. Of all the black powder sports, hunting has the most potential for adventure, is the most physically demanding and mentally stimulating. It is the closest most of us will ever get to experiencing life as it once was in frontier America. Added to this are the attractions of hunting itself: the chance to escape — at least temporarily — the concrete and glass confinements of the modern world, the opportunity to match our wits and skills against wild game, and the very real and often money-saving satisfaction of harvesting meat for the family table.

Moreover, hunting is a very natural shooting activity; it has been with us ever since the first matchlock appeared on the firearms scene. In Europe, "hunting with a firelock" was usually looked upon as a sport, but on the North American continent, it became a necessity, for the family muzzleloader also served an equally important role as the ultimate life insurance policy as well as the primary provider of food. Today in America, of course, the lure of the front-loader to the outdoorsman comes as no surprise, for the inalienable rights of our citizens to engage in gun ownership and hunting have always been a part of our heritage.

What may come as a surprise to many readers, however, is the fact that for centuries it has been the American hunter — through his wilderness knowledge, self-imposed conservation programs and monetary contributions — who has been the primary reason we still have wildlife in this country today, in spite of the cancerous spread of shopping centers, housing tracts, and overpopulation. In fact, the American hunter can claim credit for not only saving wildlife but for actually bringing some species back from the brink of extinction, and in greater numbers than ever before.

As might be expected, it is the muzzleloading hunter who can claim the closest historical ties to the conservation cause, for the first game laws in North America were created during the black powder era, in what was then considered to be a "land of plenty." Thus, in what may be a pleasant discovery to even the most knowledgeable buckskinner, it is a fact that over 250 years ago, the muzzleloading hunter was already thinking about the future of his sportsmen-heirs. Interestingly, the very first hunting regulation on this continent was established before the United States even existed: In 1677, the Colony of Connecticut created a law that banned the transportation of game across its borders. The next hunting regulation surfaced in 1738, when Virginia forebade the killing of female deer. And in the 1750's, the Massachusetts Bay Colony established specific seasons for the taking of game.

Thanks to the American hunter, not only was native wildlife saved, but entire new species were introduced. In 1882, a group of sportsmen from Oregon transplanted sixteen ringneck pheasants from China to our shores. Today, these beautifully plumed birds provide unparalleled upland hunting and tasty tablefare (not to mention fashionable feathers) in forty states.

Fortunately for all American hunters and non-hunters alike, the conservation legacy of the black powder sportsman lives on in the twentieth century.

For example, in 1900, there were only 350,000 white-tailed deer left in all of North America; practically every state had abolished its annual deer season as there were just too few animals left to hunt. Today, through hunter-sponsored game management programs, there are over sixteen million whitetails in the United States, and deer seasons have been re-established in every state. Yet, even with an annual hunter harvest of 2.1 million animals, the whitetails are overcrowding their habitat, which is shrinking thanks to encroaching urbanization.

In 1981, a herd of deer on Treasure Island, a U.S. Naval Installation near San Francisco, was left to die of overpopulation because the public would not condone a special hunting season. The hunt would have effectively thinned the herd, and at the same time, raised much needed revenue for the Fish and Game Department. But the outcry was too great to permit any of this to happen. When asked by one California official which she would prefer, to have the deer mercifully shot, or let them die a lingering death due to parasites and malnutrition, one woman stubbornly answered, "I don't want either!" You cannot reason with prejudice or ignorance. The only solution is a gradual education of the next generation before it, too, shuts off reality. Somehow, these groups must be made to understand that hunting is the only alternative to wildlife overpopulation, starvation, disease, and death by natural predators.

Ironically and sadly, in 1927, Captain Paul Curtis, shooting editor of *Field & Stream*, wrote in his book, *American Game Shooting*: "The curtain will soon ring down forever on elk shooting on the

North American continent." And "antelope...have decreased in numbers to such a discouraging degree that they will never appear on shooting lists in this country again." Morbid words from a knowledgeable outdoor writer of the time. He believed his prophecy so much that he did not even bother to list these two magnificent animals in his chapters on big game hunting species.

Fortunately for us, Captain Curtis was dead wrong in his predictions; through proper wildlife management by hunter supported efforts, our nation's elk population has grown to over a million animals and today constitutes one of North America's grandest trophies. Likewise, hunters have helped the antelope, which only numbered twelve thousand when Curtis wrote his book, to increase to more than half a million and reclaim their status as a challenging game animal.

Today, the wood duck, once on the brink of extinction, is one of the most common waterfowl in the eastern U.S., thanks solely to hunters' efforts. More recently, our native wild turkey has made a dramatic comeback from a meager, scattered flock in 1930 to 97,000 in 1954 to over 1.25 million birds today. Once relegated to the South, transplanting and habitat control in thirty states now provide sportsmen with both a spring and a fall season.

But hunters' conservation efforts have historically benefited more than just sportsmen — *all* Americans have reaped the rewards: It was a hunter — Theodore Roosevelt — who was responsible for the Reclamation Act, the National Monuments Act, and the National Conservation Commission, all of which protect wildlife; it was a hunter — Gifford Pinchot — who helped establish the U.S. Forest Service, which is responsible for preserving much of our national wilderness and bird and animal habitat; it was a hunter — J. J. Audubon — who opened the eyes of the world to the beauty of Nature's creatures; it was a group of hunters who founded Ducks Unlimited, an organization of dedicated sportsmen which has played a major role in the ongoing survival of the Northern Hemisphere's waterfowl.

Today, American hunters contribute over $225 million a year for wildlife and wilderness conservation. This money comes from state hunting license fees and federal game stamps, as well as a self-imposed 11 percent excise tax on all hunting arms and ammunition

Veteran actor Slim Pickens first "discovered" muzzleloaders while playing the part of Bill Williams, mountain man in the popular 1950's television series, "The Saga of Andy Burnett." Since then, he has been a confirmed buckskinner. A hunter since boyhood, he now ventures after game with his front-loaders. Here he holds one of his favorites, a .54 caliber copy of a Schuler swivel-breech, made for him by Lou Camilli of Albuquerque, New Mexico.

sold in this country. No such tax exists on other outdoor equipment, such as sleeping bags, fishing gear or tents, even though these items are also purchased by non-hunters who share in the same love and use of the outdoors as the hunter. But it is the *hunter* who pays the costs of reforestation, wildlife restocking, and the preservation of breeding marshes and ponds. In fact, it is sobering to contemplate the disastrous fate of our natural resources — game and land alike — should the hunter ever be banned from his sport. Where else would our nation's game management money come from? More taxes? An already overburdened federal budget? Sporadic contributions? Our wildlife agencies would soon dry up and die like the very land and animals they were empowered to protect. Considering the fact that roughly thirty to fifty million dollars is spent by various anti-hunting factions each year to try and outlaw our cherished sport, one cannot help but wonder how much better it would be if these dollars were put *towards* conservation instead of trying to fight it.

That's why, whenever people ask me what they can do to help protect wildlife, I always answer, "Buy a hunting license." And if they say, "But I don't hunt," I reply, "Then you'd better buy a duck stamp, too."

After all, the hunter shares a common bond with the rest of Nature's admirers, be they bird watchers, backpackers, painters, or photographers. As Americans, we have all inherited a tremendous responsibility — the ongoing preservation of our natural wildlife. Yet it is the hunter, through his deeper understanding of Nature, who has assumed the primary responsibility for the protection of that inheritance.

Unlike many other nations, every American is born with the right to hunt; whether or not an individual chooses to exercise that right is a personal decision. But for those who do, the election to refine that right by using a muzzleloader brings us back to the very roots of our beginning as a freedom-seeking people, whether it be freedom from the tyrannical rule of a distant and uncompromising government, or freedom to break from the bonds of civilization and head towards an unknown adventure that awaits beyond the next mountain.

[13]

What shooter cannot pick up a Kentucky or plains rifle and be captivated by the romance and adventure that silently speaks to us from the lines of the barrel, stock and trigger guard? How often have we dreamt by the fireplace, the living room window, or even at the office desk, of faraway hunts, real or imagined, in which we proudly carried a charged and ready muzzleloader as we slowly stalked through an autumn-tinged forest, breathing in the crisp sting of cold morning air, our senses alert to every movement and sound? Two hundred years ago that snap of a twig could just as easily have been a Tory; one hundred years ago that odd-shaped shadow might have warned us of Blackfeet nearby. But these are the only differences that separate the muzzleloading hunter of today with his counterpart of a century or two ago. For the most part, our guns are designed the same; the methods of loading and shooting are the same; our love of the wilderness and admiration for the game we hunt is the same. Indeed, the black powder hunter of today is as close as the twentieth century will let us get to the past. In a sense, we have become a part of our country's living history.

However, there is more to black powder hunting than just nostalgia. There has to be, or else we might eventually be content to merely hang our smokepole on the fireplace wall and gaze at it longingly as we gradually drift off into a sour mash-induced state of euphoria. But then, what would cause a theoretically sane man or woman to turn away from some of the finest products modern firearms technology has produced, and to exchange those scoped, lightweight, fast-shooting, far-reaching, multiple-shot zippers for their ultimate antithesis, a heavy gun with an exposed hammer, capable of firing once or at best twice a minute, and at a range that is severely limited by the use of open sights and the shooter's natural ability to see his game?

The answer can be found in what I have often referred to as "The Black Powder Challenge."

Most hunters—those men and women who harvest game in accordance with the written laws of the land and the unwritten code of good sportsmanship—are a noble breed. But those individuals who, in addition to seeking the call of the wilderness, also choose to answer the black powder challenge, enter a world of their own; a world that is unique in today's society, a world that demands the utmost performance from both the hunter and his muzzleloader.

One does not necessarily have to come from the smokeless powder ranks to hear the call of that challenge, but many do. Others enter the camp of the muzzleloading hunter with their hands untainted by the brass casings of the self-contained metallic cartridge gun. Either way, those who hear the call and answer its challenge are bonded together by a common philosophy, even though their backgrounds or cultures or jobs or incomes may be as dissimilar as the patterns of individual snowflakes. But their reasons for meeting the challenge are always the same — a quest for individuality, a desire to put more sport in the hunt, and a search for the qualities that formed the framework of the American frontier. And by virtue of the first two elements, the third is automatically attained.

Putting motivations and goals aside, firing a black powder gun is one of the most fun-filled and relaxing of all recreational endeavors. But as relaxing as it may be, ironically, black powder hunting can also be the most demanding, for in order to be effective, the muzzleloading hunter must perfect his skills of stalking, wildlife knowledge, marksmanship, and patience. Of course, any wartbrained idiot can yank a freshly purchased front-loader out of the box, pour powder and ball down the barrel without bothering to see where or how the gun shoots, and stumble off into the woods, where he could conceivably wander around for weeks without realizing anything was amiss. It's a great way to avoid the inconvenience of filling out your game tag each year and lugging all that meat home.

But for the hunter who decides to take the time and dedication to answer the black powder challenge, the rewards are great: He learns to make every pull of the trigger a sure and accurate one. Whereas his cartridge-shooting counterpart might occasionally be tempted to unleash a volley of shots at a dimly outlined game animal, the muzzleloading hunter holds his fire until he is well within range and is sure of his target, even if it means passing up a shot. After all, it takes an average black powder hunter anywhere from thirty seconds to a full minute to reload his rifle in the field, and that means a missed first shot is your last shot, at least for that particular animal. Thus, although a muzzleloading gun may only speak once during a hunt, the fall of the hammer, flash of fire, and billowing cloud of smoke is usually a signal that the pathfinder has filled his tag. And it only takes one successful muzzleloading hunt to instill confidence and satisfaction in a hunter that is virtually unknown in any other form of shooting. Not only did you carry a muzzleloader that represents a period of history with which you personally identify, but you determined the proper load yourself, personally poured the powder, rammed home the charge, and succeeded in harvesting game exactly as it was done by our nation's frontiersmen over a century ago. And finally, there is always that euphoric swell of pride when describing a successful hunt, when you pause for the inevitable question, "What did you shoot him with?", and you are able to answer, "I took him with a muzzleloader!"

Perhaps that is the reason that wild game, no matter how my wife cooks it, always seems to taste just a little bit better when I've taken it with a black powder firearm. Once, while visiting friends in Kansas City, I was treated to a wonderfully prepared elk steak dinner in a skytop restaurant that specialized in "exotic" wild game. Pound for pound, that meal, including cocktails, wine, and tip, probably cost about the same as the five-point bull I shot a few years later in the Rocky Mountains of Wyoming. That particular elk dinner also had a lofty view, for we were camped about 10,000 feet up in a high country meadow. Of course, our packer's tent had no starched tablecloth and no wine (although I do remember a bottle of nondescript bourbon being nearby). But the elk meat I ate with a wrangler late that night, after riding two-and-a-half hours back to camp in a bone-chilling rainstorm, was one of the most memorable meals I have ever put a fork to. And I knew the elk meat was fresh, for I had shot that noble creature earlier in the day with a .54 caliber black powder Sharps. But then, the pungent odor of sulfur smoke, when mixed with the fresh pine-laden aroma of a rain-soaked forest, has always been a powerful seasoning that would enhance any meal.

But getting your game is not the main ingredient necessary for an enjoyable hunt. In fact, it should be remembered that most hunters — muzzleloading and otherwise — come back home dirty, smelly, tired — and empty-handed. But they have had a good time! In fact, one of my most memorable hunts was a ten-day horseback trek after black bear in Wyoming. I was writing an article on Mountain Man

Long an avid outdoorsman, Charlton Heston discovered the lure of the muzzle-loading hunter while on location in Wyoming, filming (appropriately enough), *The Mountain Men*. Photo courtesy of Columbia Pictures.

hunting for one of the leading gun magazines, and carried not one, but two .54 caliber Hawkens in twin saddle scabbards, *a la* Jeremiah Johnson. During my week-and-a-half session in the saddle, I rode through some of the most spectacular scenery I had ever seen: lofty granite crags covered with perpetual snow, skies that were so intensely blue they looked almost black, grass-carpeted valleys few men had ever seen, ice-clear streams bubbling out of moss-covered rocks, and an abundance of wildlife that included bighorn sheep, elk, deer, eagles, and moose. But no bear. In fact, the only time I fired my two rifles was to clear the bores prior to my plane trip home. But nonetheless, that particular hunting trip shall be etched forever upon my memory as one of the grandest adventures of my life, for I had been privileged to have ridden through one of nature's most hallowed and hidden temples.

For me, the thrill of a hunt lies first in the anticipation. I usually start thinking about a hunt a full year in advance, reading books, sending for catalogs, studying maps, checking equipment, and becoming a general burden to my poor wife, who must listen to my diatribes on what gun to use, what bullet to cast, and when the moon will come up. Next, of course, is the actual hunt itself, but that experience is usually so fleeting, I never really enjoy the full measure of my wilderness ventures until I get back, when I have time to reflect upon them, usually in the company of friends and after being sufficiently fortified with a few ounces of 90 proof.

Naturally, getting the game gives one a tremendous lift to morale and adds considerable flavor to any hunting yarn, especially when the animal is charging (as most of them do after a few times around the cocktail circuit) and is near record-book size. ("The reason there's only 30 pounds of meat on this deer is that the rest of him was all muscle...!")

But lining up the sights and pulling the trigger is performed in such a fleeting moment in time, it seems to lose all perspective in proportion to the other elements that make up a good hunt. On one occasion not very long ago, I was big game hunting in the rugged foothills east of Paso Robles in California. This is cattle country and I had taken a fair amount of ribbing about my "old timey guns" from the local drovers in the area. But on the first day of the hunt, I shot a hefty Black Russian boar (he really *was* charging!). And two days later, I stalked a nice forked-horn buck until I got within 30 feet of him, whereupon I commenced to make a rather spectacular one-shot kill. But the best time of that hunt for me was afterwards, sitting on a case of Coors in the cooling shed and gazing at my two skinned-out animals as I thought about the heat and dust of the day, anticipated my wife's pleasantly surprised reaction when she would learn of my success, contemplated cleaning my rifle and smoking a pipe that night, and a hundred other thoughts that cross a hunter's mind in such a setting. In fact, this is the first time I have ever written about that particular hunt, for it has always struck me as being too much of a "gun writer's yarn": two shots and two animals in three days — Ha! But, the fact that it happened was reward enough for me. And I suspect my thoughts that day were the same as another muzzleloading hunter of long ago, who had a similar successful experience. Likewise, I have since seen the emotions I felt while riding through the Rockies expressed by other writers of an earlier time; most notably George Ruxton (*Ruxton of the Rockies*, 1848) and William Baille-Grohman (*Camps in the Rockies*, 1882).

And so it is that the muzzleloading hunter of today is the culmination of the sporting world's past, present, and future. His memory is enriched with the knowledge of the past; he is acquainted with the history of his guns and of the deerstalkers, mountain men and scouts who carried them. Thus, he has the unique ability to choose any era in the past 600 years — from matchlock to percussion — in which to pursue his sport, a privilege normally only afforded to science fiction time travelers. And even though the black powder rifles, pistols, and shotguns of today may look like those weapons of his frontier forebearers, the metal is stronger, the variety and accessibility of the guns are greater, and the equipment is often better. Likewise, the muzzleloading hunter's knowledge is more quickly learned, for he has the world's entire shooting and hunting history from which to draw, a legacy left to him by his pioneer predecessors. Additionally and somewhat ironically, this is the first time in shooting history that special "black powder seasons" have been specified for hunters, even though muzzleloaders can be used to hunt with in all fifty states during regular "metallic cartridge" game seasons. It is a unique situation, but a welcomed one that gives clear evidence of black powder hunting's popularity and growth. (A listing of those

states offering special muzzleloading seasons will be found in the back of this book.)

And of the future? That is the most valuable heritage of all, for in his hands, by his deeds, the black powder sportsman of today has the priceless ability to blaze a trail for all future generations to follow, a path that is always there to be discovered by any hunter who wishes to answer the black powder challenge. Muzzleloading hunting is a timeless adventure that shall exist as long as there is romance in our souls, and men are free to own firearms of their choosing and can find solace in the wilderness. Thereby do we perpetuate the hunter's heritage.

Consequently, I have always felt it was a disservice to say that the muzzleloading hunter of the twentieth century walks in the shadows of men like Crockett, Boone, Carson and Bridger . . . rather, he walks *alongside* them.

CHAPTER TWO

◀·▶

THE HUNTING RIFLE

B est buddies and brothers-in-law aside, the most trustworthy hunting partner you will ever have is your black powder rifle. Whether honorably exhibited in a gun rack over the fireplace or casually leaning against a cabin wall, it is a source of constant reassurance and brings back memories of good times past. Carried at your side, it holds the promise of another memorable hunt. At your command, it will speak with authority. In times of peril, it can protect you from danger. But in return for all this loyalty, the rifle demands attention and respect.

The muzzleloading hunter of the twentieth century has fallen heir to a vast assortment of black powder rifles, all of which are direct descendants from the past. In fact, it is difficult to tell some of today's guns, such as the Tennessee Valley Arms rifles and the Shiloh Sharps, from their 150-year-old relatives, even when viewed alongside the originals. Other rifles, most notably the Thompson/Center Renegade and the Sile Hunter, sport refinements such as coil mainsprings, adjustable sights and modern stock designs that make them unlike anything ever to spit lead during the nineteenth century. Yet without a doubt, any one of today's black powder shoulder weapons, if transported back 100 or 200 years, would be instantly recognized for what it is: a muzzleloading hunting rifle.

Your rifle will probably be the single most expensive item you will ever buy in the pursuit of this sport. Therefore, its selection should be made with care and with caution. Years ago, when the first replicas began coming out, I made the mistake of buying a cheap imported Belgian flintlock. It looked pretty sitting in that war surplus store's gun rack, and it was super-affordable. If buying that gun was not bad enough, I made an even bigger mistake when I took it out to the desert to shoot it for the first time at an unsuspecting jackrabbit. The gun promptly blew up in my hands. I never did see that rabbit again, but I found the ramrod sticking out of a mesquite bush ten feet in front of me and the trigger guard was left dangling from my finger. The bright, shiny lock had blown clean out from the right side of the stock, making me thankful that I was not left-handed. Luckily, I was not injured. That was the only adverse black powder shooting incident I have ever had, because I learned an important lesson that day: Never trust your life or your hunting success to a cheap or poorly made grade of gun; always buy the very best you can afford. You may have to save a little more money and wait a little longer for your rifle, but you will end up with a better investment and will have a muzzleloader that will become a reliable hunting partner.

That is not to say you should necessarily limit yourself to just one gun, although many hunters, once they have found the "ultimate rifle," will stay with it throughout their hunting lifetimes. Some hunters, like myself, prefer to have a variety of rifles to select from; some days just seem right for shooting a flintlock, while others demand a percussion. Dangerous game might cause me to consider a gun that offers a fast shooting advantage, such as the Kodiak double rifle. Other times I may not feel like taking my .58 CVA Big Bore out after cottontails and it is nice to have a .36 Mowrey Squirrel Rifle to pluck from the rack.

For the one-gun hunter, I should point out that you can shoot small game with a large caliber rifle. I once shot a golden-mantled meadow mouse in the wilds of Wyoming, using a .54 Hawken, a Butler Creek Poly-Patch and 15 grains of FFG. No ball. The range was 10 feet, the creature had reared up on his hind legs ready to charge, and it was a clean, one-shot kill. Jackson Hole taxidermist Norris Brown even mounted the head for me, as it was my first Boone and Crockett mouse.

In spite of the front-loader's versatility in varying powder charge and projectile to meet the various shooting conditions and creatures the hunter may encounter, it is still a far better idea to match the caliber up with the game you plan to pursue. Most mass-produced muzzleloading rifles come in the following calibers: .36 (ideal for small game hunting); .50 (the most popular of all, yet the very minimum any hunter should consider for medium-sized animals such as deer and wild boar); .54 (the ideal big game hunting caliber, offering a compromise between bone-crushing knockdown power and accuracy); and .58 (the largest mass-produced rifle caliber and one that is suitable for the biggest game on any continent).

Large game animals, such as elk, buffalo, and moose should not be hunted with anything less than .54 caliber, with .58 being preferable. In black powder hunting, especially when after dangerous

Mike Powasnick, president of Trail Guns Armory, decided to field test his Kodiak double rifle on safari, where the guns first saw fame during the 19th Century. He is shown here with his recordbook Cape Buffalo, which he dropped using loads of 140 grains of Pyrodex and a 700-grain conical bullet.

game such as bear, there is no such thing as being overgunned. Of course, there is an infinite variety of other calibers available from custom barrelmakers and gunsmiths, normally ranging from .31 to .62, but when getting into these maverick loadings, the hunter may encounter problems in obtaining the correct size bullet mould, precast conical slugs, and loading/cleaning accoutrements. The muzzleloading hunter who sometimes finds himself far from home or on the eve of a hunt looking for extra balls or a loading jag, is advised to select from one or more of the four standard calibers listed above. They are adequate for all hunting needs and have been for over 150 years.

Using my .54 Sharps Gemmer, I felled this trophy bull elk with a single shot.

Unless you live in a state such as Massachusetts, which requires smoothbores for black powder hunting, most muzzleloading sportsmen use rifles rather than muskets. Even though a musket can throw a heavier ball (usually ranging from .69 to .75 caliber) and is quicker to reload due to its smooth bore (which can also double as a scattergun when loaded with shot), that same unrifled tube only provides marginal accuracy at ranges that cease to become effective beyond 50 yards. The rifle, on the other hand, is capable of excellent hunting accuracy out to 100 yards and beyond. This combination of greater range and accuracy makes the rifle the only practical choice for the hunter. (See Chapter Five for more information on ballistics and killing power.) Actually, the rifled bullet will travel well beyond the 100-yard hunting limit. Long-range Creedmore matches were popular in the last century, when targets were shot at 500, 800, and even 1,000 yards. But killing power of the projectile drops off dramatically at these extreme distances, and they are definitely not for black powder hunting.

Today the muzzleloading hunter is fortunate in being able to select from more styles and variations of rifles than have existed at any time since the close of the Victorian era. Grandad never had it so good, and our choices today no doubt rival those of Great-grandad. And it is a fact that today's black powder rifles cost *less* than those of 150 years ago, on a dollar-for-dollar value, with inflation averaged in. In the early 1800's, a good, serviceable hunting rifle cost the hunter anywhere from $4 to $10, which was often more than a month's wages for the average man back then, if he had any wages at all. (In America's early agrarian society, most men were self-sufficient, and often had no real need for money, making the purchase of a long rifle even more difficult, unless it could be obtained by bartering crops or meat.) By the 1850's, the price of the best big bored half-stock hunting rifle had risen to $16, with the fancier versions bringing $37, which equaled two months' wages for the average worker. Good guns were hard to get. What's more, the metal of those days was soft, requiring that a rifle be occasionally "freshened out," or re-bored to a larger caliber in order to cut sharper lands and grooves of the rifling, after it had been worn smooth through constant use.

Today's black powder hunter has none of these problems; the steels in his guns are among the toughest obtainable, and "freshening out" old, worn-out rifling is a practice that is rarely performed anymore. The gun you buy today should last a couple of lifetimes with no major repair work being required. Moreover, most of the excellent quality rifles we will be discussing can be acquired for a weekly paycheck. Of course, fancier guns with custom work will cost more, but usually the price will not exceed a two months' salary for such craftsmanship (which often approaches the collector category, and the custom hunting rifle is often worth more, even after a few years' hard use, than the owner originally paid for it).

Basically, there are three different styles of muzzleloading rifles from which today's hunter may choose. First, there are the civilian or sporting guns, such as the Kentuckies and half-stock plains rifles, historical arms originally designed for both protection and hunting and which are closely linked with the romance of our country's expansion. Second are the military rifles, which have been extremely popular with Civil War reenactment groups, but have ironically been underrated as hunting guns. Yet their rugged designs, excellent sights and unbreakable steel ramrods make them ideal for this purpose. Finally we have the modern muzzleloaders: those guns created within the latter part of this century specifically to fill a void in the black powder hunting scene by updating age-old designs.

In addition to these three basic types of hunting rifles, the sportsman may also select from two distinct black powder ignition systems, flintlock or percussion. Because of the importance your rifle will play in your game-getting ability, a bit of discussion is warranted on both.

The flintlock was popular as a hunting arm throughout the 1700's and well into the middle of the nineteenth century. Its lock consists of a hammer, or "cock," with open, adjustable jaws, like a vise. Into these jaws a pre-shaped wedge of flint, wrapped with a tab of leather to help hold it, is placed. The jaws are then tightened down upon the leather-covered flint. When the hammer is cocked and the trigger pulled, the hammer flies forward, causing the edge of the flint to strike a steel plate, referred to as the frizzen. This causes (if your flint is shaped right and is firmly held by the hammer) a great number of sparks. Upon being struck with the flint, the frizzen springs back, revealing a shallow metal "pan" filled with fast-burning FFFFG black powder. If any of the sparks strike this priming powder, it ignites with a *whoosh*, sending a flash of fire through a touch hole bored through the side of the barrel, which thereby ignites the main charge in the breech, and the gun fires. As complicated as this may all sound, it occurs within a split second on a well-timed lock and can make shooting your rifle a rather exciting event. However, because the crucial igniting charge is located on the exterior of the lock, touching off a flinter can be somewhat disconcerting to a hunter who does not feel comfortable with all that flash and smoke erupting so close to his face. In addition, the open ignition system of a flintlock can create an extreme fire hazard during the dry months of early fall. The firelock itself is subject to failure due to a chipped or misaligned flint, worn frizzen, inadequate priming charge, or failure of the exploding FFFFG to share any of its fire with the main charge in the barrel. It is an all-too-common sight to see a flintlock shooter "fire" his lock, but not his rifle, in which case he must re-prime and start over. This is only moderately embarrassing on the target range; in the field, it can be the sole reason for coming home empty-handed. The flintlock's design also makes it extremely sensitive to weather; firing a flinter in wind or rain is a true exercise in frustration—I know, I've been there. A sudden gust of wind can blow your priming powder out of the flashpan during a crucial moment of the hunt, and many of the locks are susceptible to rain. Given all these variables, the outdoorsman who takes any game, big or small, furred or feathered, with a flintlock has ample reason to be proud. Because a flinter requires a lot of extra attention, I would recommend it only for the hunter who has already had some experience with black powder rifles, or who is not planning to take it on that once-in-a-lifetime big game hunt in which he may get only one shot at a trophy animal. In the excitement of the hunt, some of the flintlock's fine points of maintenance may be overlooked.

A far more practical means of setting off black powder for the hunter is the caplock, or percussion rifle. First introduced to the shooting scene in 1820, the caplock remained *the* favored firearm during the fur trade, and throughout the Civil War and western expansion years, right up to and beyond the advent of the cartridge rifle. Its lock consists of a solid hammer which, when fired, strikes an expendable explosive "cap" which has been fitted onto a small, short tube referred to as the nipple. The flash from the cap goes through the hole in the nipple and directly into the main powder charge in the barrel. As you may have already surmised, the percussion rifle is somewhat faster than a flintlock, more reliable, and it makes it possible to continue a hunt during inclement weather that would render a flintlock useless. Of course, you cannot start a campfire with a caplock, as you can with a flinter. And if you forget your caps, you might as well turn your hunting rifle into a club. But these are minor drawbacks compared to the greater advantages of the percussion gun for the hunter, whether he be experienced buckskinner or neophyte pilgrim. It is my steadfast recommendation for a first-time hunting gun, and even the confirmed flintlock shooter should have at least one percussion rifle in his rack to use as a backup. The only exception to this would be in a state such as Pennsylvania, which has a flintlock-only rule to hamper its primitive hunts. (No, it really doesn't make sense, but it is the law.)

No matter what type of lock or style of hunting rifle you ultimately select, it should be devoid of reflective metalwork that could spook game; aside from sunlight glistening off water, the only shiny items emitting flashes of light in the wilderness are manmade. They are foreign to their natural surroundings and act as warning beacons to wildlife, announcing your presence as sure as a sneeze and as quick as a cough. That means the optimum hunting rifle should have dark wood, and brown or blued metalwork. Some of the otherwise better quality hunting guns sport pewter nosecaps or brass trigger guards. These items should either be chemically oxidized, allowed to tarnish to a deep nonreflective brown, or covered with masking tape during the hunt. Highly polished brass patchboxes and shiny silver inlays are fine for presentation guns, match rifles, and wall hangers, but they have no place on a hunting rifle, which must blend into its surroundings as much as the hunter.

Most rifles come with "set" triggers: that is, a single or double trigger that can be adjusted to fire with very little pressure when it is "set." Normally, this feature is of more benefit to the target shooter, although I have used set triggers on long range shots and on those occasions when I was stillhunting and had plenty of time to aim. For the hunter on horseback or who stalks his game, the set trigger can be dangerous, as an accidental stumble with a cocked rifle could fire it. I have adjusted the trigger pull on most of my hunting rifles to 2½ pounds, which is more than adequate, although many shooters prefer heavier pulls of 5 to 7 pounds. For fast shots this is fine, but I find the heavier pull tends to build up tension, raising the possibility of the hunter flinching and throwing his shot.

All muzzleloading hunting rifles come with traditional open sights. Depending on which gun you select, the sights will be either "fixed" (an age-old method by which front and rear sights are shaped with a small file and "drifted" left or right with a brass hammer to finally bring them on target) or "adjustable" (whereby windage and elevation is set by turning a screw on the rear sight). Either of these sight arrangements is suitable, although I prefer the fixed sight due to the fact that once it is "on target" it stays on target — usually. There are exceptions to everything and I recall taking a lengthy fall down a steep, gravelly slope while trying to outrun a whitetail in an effort to get a clear shot from the crest of a mountain ridge. I held on to my Hawken all the way down and we both landed on our front ends. I had a few bruises that eventually healed, but the silver blade front sight was bent almost in two and I never was able to get the sight perfectly straightened out. It would have been great for shooting around corners if I had laid the rifle on its side. Rather than replace it, I decided it gave more character to that old gun, and I eventually learned to shoot with it. I bagged a blacktailed deer with that octagon-barrelled half-stock a few years later.

Most open rear sights are shaped in a traditional Rocky Mountain Buckhorn — a deep crescent curve that is still my favorite after all these years — or a more conservative, flat-topped, semi-buckhorn. Either sight is good for hunting in thick woods or dim light, as long as the notch in the rear sight is deep enough to be seen. You may have to do some filing, even on adjustable sights, in this case. Front sights are normally a thin or medium-sized silver blade, but a few of the rifles have a thicker post with a round bead on top, an ideal arrangement for the hunter. In Chapter Five, there are photographs of front and rear sights made by Marble's, Lyman, and Tedd Cash, which you may want to consider as possible replacements for your rifle's sights. However, most of the sights on the better-grade rifles are more than adequate if you will take the time to learn to use them.

The three basic projectiles available to muzzleloading hunters are the hollow-based Mini, the solid Maxi, and the traditional round ball.

Every muzzleloader made today has the barrel rifled in one of two ways: either a slow twist (such as one twist of rifling in 66 inches) or a fast twist (one twist in 48 inches is more or less standard). The slow twist barrels will shoot more accurately with a patched round ball, while the fast twist guns handle the conical Mini, Maxi or R.E.A.L. bullets best. Both round ball and conical will kill game, but the round ball has a tendency to pass through body tissue unless it hits a bone, in which case it flattens out admirably. The conical slug has greater shock power and normally expands whether or not it hits bone. It is not, however, as accurate as a round ball, although it is capable of more-than-adequate hunting accuracy out to 100 yards and is easier to load, requiring no patch. I prefer them for big game hunting and have used conical slugs in slow twist barrels with excellent results, even though the "round ball" barrel may cause the conical's group to spread as wide as 6 to 10 inches at 100 yards; less when fired at a closer range. A more detailed explanation of the round ball versus conical debate (a popular one among buckskinners) can be found in Chapter Five. It should be noted that Minis and Maxis build up greater pressure within the chamber of your rifle (you will experience a heavier recoil) so if you hunt with these conical projectiles, it is even more imperative that only top quality rifles be used. In any case, do not let the twist of the bore stop you from buying the rifle you want; good hunting loads can be worked up for any well-made muzzleloader.

As long as the criteria for a hunting rifle are followed, there is no such thing as a "right" or a "wrong" choice. You will unquestionably pick the correct rifle because it will be an extension of your own hunting personality, based upon design, price, and the period in history with which you identify. To help review the possibilities, I have selected some of the best rifles available to the muzzleloading hunter today. In addition to interviewing most of the manufacturers, I have personally examined, tested, and fired every one of the rifles listed in this chapter and have hunted with most of them. Sadly, there were more guns that did not make this book than there are in it. That is because the muzzleloading hunter's criteria leave little room for compromise. Reasons for omission include poor workmanship or unsuitability of gun design for hunting. A few otherwise excellent guns were eliminated for this reason. I also have omitted individual custom gun makers, as they usually turn out two or three guns a year and therefore do not have a product the muzzleloading hunter can easily obtain. No book such as this can ever be complete. Because of the continuing growth of black powder hunting, there are new rifles being introduced every year, and we have an enjoyable obligation to keep ourselves posted on the latest muzzleloaders that are suitable for the hunter's camp. But the following rifles have already proven themselves and are indeed worthy of the title, A Hunting Rifle.

Let's start with the earliest guns first, mainly the plainer-grade hunting Kentuckies. They are more popularly called Poor Boy rifles, due to their lack of shiny ornamental brass. This very feature makes these slim, long-barreled guns, with their greater sight radius, ideal for the hunter. Of all the Kentucky-styled rifles that I have fired, I would give top marks to Dixie Gun Works' Tennessee Mountain Rifle, in terms of value for dollars spent. Authentically patterned after the long rifle used by hunters and frontiersmen of the Appalachian Mountains from about 1785 through 1850, this .50 caliber,

My "Big Medicine Gun," a custom .54 Plains Rifle, made for me by John Speak.

Dixie Gun Works' Tennessee Mountain Rifle combines authentic design with an affordable price.

41½-inch barrel arm is available in *either* percussion or flintlock. This rifle is also one of the few production guns that comes in both right- and left-hand models. Both locks are historically proper for the rifle's design, depending where in history the shooter places himself, and his preference for ignition.

On one of my trips to Tennessee, I visited with the folks at Dixie Gun Works and had the opportunity to test-fire Tennessee Mountain Rifle No. 4 — one of the first ones produced — and found its flintlock to be exceptionally fast. This is especially significant since, due to a forgetful lack of FFFFG, we primed the pan with FFFG powder! Since that time, I have acquired TMR No. 87, with which I fired a five-shot string using 70 grains of FFFG black powder backing a patched round ball. Lock time was instantaneous, and I produced a group measuring slightly over 1 inch at 50 yards. That is true match-quality shooting for a hunting gun.

Accuracy was helped by the double-set triggers, which I had adjusted to a crisp 9 ounces of pull. That's just too fine for hunting (and I have since backed them off to a safer and more practical 2½ pounds), but it does indicate the potential accuracy of this well-built arm. Similar results were obtained when I unscrewed the vent-hole in the barrel and screwed in the percussion nipple and lock. All metal parts are nicely browned, and the cherrywood stock is authentically stained. Like many backwoods rifles used throughout the Mississippi Valley, the Tennessee Mountain Rifle has no patchbox, but instead features a "grease-hole" in the right-hand side of the stock. I initially filled this clean-cut depression with my traditional mixture of mutton tallow and beeswax, but frankly I kept getting the stuff all over my shirtsleeve. Consequently, for hunting use, I recommend pregreased patches, or patchless conical slugs. Let the grease-hole remain decorative. The Tennessee Mountain Rifle may be ordered directly from Dixie with your choice of locks. Should you wish to change ignition systems, an extra lock in either flint or percussion can be purchased. The gun is also available in kit form if you have a few simple tools and feel like building your own. Either way, kit or ready-made, Dixie's Tennessee Mountain Rifle is an excellent bargain for the hunter.

Another excellent early-style long gun is the Tennessee Rifle made by Tennessee Valley Arms. (Ever wonder why all the good hunters' Kentuckies come from Tennessee?) This ultra-fine quality front-loader borders on the custom gun category, as each is handmade to your order. That means you will probably have a six-month wait to get your TVA rifle, but it will be worth it! You can save both

My Tennessee Valley Arms Squirrel Rifle "Liz" is in .36 caliber, but any size bore is available, from .32 to .62, in either flintlock or percussion.

time and money by ordering TVA's Tennessee Rifle Kit. However, not being one of today's better craftsmen (I have always sworn I would never live in, drive, or shoot anything that I personally built), I elected to have Jack Garner and Ernie Tidwell of TVA put my rifle together: a classic .36 Squirrel gun I have named Liz. (This might be a good place to mention that TVA and Mowrey — another firm we shall be discussing — are the only riflemakers producing small caliber squirrel rifles on a regular basis; all the other guns are in the big game category.) The standard TVA Tennessee Rifle comes in .45 caliber, although for a few dollars more you can have *your choice* of calibers, ranging from .32 to .62. The lock is either flint or percussion. The standard-grade curly maple stock has a far prettier grain than I would expect on a hunting rifle, and the butt has a horn heel and a steel toe plate, rather than the usual buttplate. All metalwork is browned. The trigger is a single set, which means the gun cannot be fired without setting the trigger for a preadjusted pull. Because of this, I would recommend setting the pull slightly heavier than normal, to prevent the gun from accidentally discharging during a fast reflex move by the hunter. (With any rifle, it is always a good idea to keep your finger out of the trigger guard until you are ready to shoot.) Other options for the TVA rifle include extra fancy curly maple, cherry, or walnut for the stock, a choice of different locks and barrels, a left-hand action, browned steel patchbox, and practically any other extra you are willing to pay for. Whether you purchase their standard rifle or a custom deluxe, you will be obtaining a wonderfully accurate hunting gun. I have a standard Douglas barrel on my .36 , and firing 35 grains of FFFG at 50 yards, I placed two shots within the same hole; not bad for a muzzleloader that is authentically beautiful as well.

Leaving the Leatherstocking-inspired glamour of the long rifle, let us shift our sights west to another extremely popular style of hunting gun, the classic Hawken Rifle. So much magic does the Hawken name carry, that today approximately half of the muzzleloaders on the market are christened with that designation, whether they look anything like the original or not. However, four of today's top hunting rifles are almost duplicate images of the famed St. Louis rifle made by Sam and Jake Hawken for the Rocky Mountain fur trade. This famous rifle continued to be used well beyond the moun-

Both the Dixie and TVA "Poor Boys" come with optional interchangeable ignition systems. This is the Tennessee Mountain Rifle.

tain man era, lasting throughout the big game hunting years of the 1860's, '70's, and '80's, in which the big bored, hard-shooting Hawken had far more power than any of the newfangled "self-contained, metallic, cartridge guns." Although probably fewer than three thousand Hawken rifles were ever actually built, in its day it was probably *the* standard by which all other hunting guns were judged. In many ways, it still is.

The first Hawken we shall look at is made by Navy Arms, and holds the distinction of being the only such gun that is completely crafted in the U.S. It is actually referred to as the Ithaca/Navy Hawken Rifle, and is available in either flintlock or percussion, but in both cases comes with a half-stock and double-set triggers. With the exception of a pewter nosecap and wedge escutcheons, all metalwork is browned. The gun has a 32-inch barrel rifled for round ball and comes in .50 or .54 caliber, of which I would opt for the larger bore due to its greater versatility on all sizes of game. Both flint and caplock versions of the Ithaca/Navy Hawken, in either caliber, are available in kit form. Using a patched round ball and a proven load of 80 grains of FFG, I fired a five-shot string at 50 yards that measured 2½ inches; the first three shots were with set trigger and clustered around 1½ inches; the last two were without setting the trigger. All were shot offhand, a practical exercise as that is how most hunting shots are fired. Besides its remarkable accuracy and handsome looks, the Ithaca/Navy Hawken has another plus found all too infre-

The Ithaca/Navy Hawken, shown here, and the Lyman Great Plains Rifle are the only two Plains Rifles available in both flint and percussion.

Allen Arms makes this extremely rugged Jed Smith Hawken.

quently with today's muzzleloaders: it comes with an excellent booklet that tells you all you'll ever want to know about the history, loading, and shooting of your rifle.

Another authentically Hawken-styled rifle which has come on the hunter's scene, and which I consider ideal for big game, is Allen Arms' "Jed Smith" Hawken Rifle, a .54 caliber, half-stock plains gun that is as rugged as it is hard-shooting. The Allen Arms version is authentic in almost every detail, from the browned furniture to the double-set triggers to the black walnut stock, which is made thicker in the wrist and fore-end to help absorb recoil. On one of my Rocky Mountain bear hunts on horseback, I found that the thicker wood of the Allen Arms Hawken made it easier to carry across the pommel of my saddle. Original mountain rifles often exhibit a concave depression along the bottom of their stocks, and it seems this chunkier area of the Allen Arms gun was designed to offset this situation somewhat by providing more wood to wear away. The thick walnut stock indicated that it would take substantial wear and tear over the years. On this same hunt, during one memorable 30-mile ride back to camp in a blizzard, I arrived with my frosty Jed Smith Hawken in its saddle scabbard, looking more like a snowcone than a rifle. Temperatures had dropped to 15 degrees, and both my gun and myself were completely encrusted in ice and snow. Naturally I was concerned about the ability of my muzzleloader to fire. Under these adverse conditions, it is advisable to clear the barrel and put in a fresh load for the next day's hunt. If there is no nearby game to spook, the easiest way is to fire the gun—if it will fire (usually you will have to pull the ball with a worm and scoop out the wet powder).

After dismounting, I cracked the Hawken free from its ice-covered scabbard, walked a few yards away from the horses, cocked the hammer and pulled the double-set triggers. To my pleasant surprise, the gun roared into the frigid night air as sure and quick as if it had been a warm summer's day. Needless to say, I was filled with the utmost confidence for this particular muzzleloader as a reliable gun for the hunter who must venture into remote areas under the most adverse conditions.

There are three minor faults I found on this Hawken, but fortunately two of them are cosmetic, not functional. First, although most of the metalwork is browned, for some inexplicable reason, the hammer on my Hawken was *blued*. Second, the pewter nosecap, while attractive, tends to reflect light, and I would suggest that the hunter using this rifle cover the nosecap with a non-reflective masking tape, or chemically tarnish it to a dull, aged-looking gray. The third discrepancy is in its caliber. Although touted as a .54, the bore is actually .526, which means you will be using some new words if you have to reload in a hurry. Actually, the muzzle of this particular rifle is "choked" tighter than the rest of the bore, a situation often encountered on some premium barrels used by custom black powder riflesmiths. While this constriction does provide slightly greater accuracy, it also makes starting your patched ball or greased Mini bullet somewhat slower. Maxis and R.E.A.L. bullets are almost impossible to get past the choke without some hard raps on the short starter. I ended up carrying a small plastic-head hammer with me for quickly starting the Mini down the bore; once past the muzzle, the ball rammed down with ease. I have even considered having a gunsmith take about 4 inches off the barrel, which would get rid of the choke and reduce the barrel length to a handy 28 inches, but I am leery of tampering with the wonderful accuracy of the gun.

The Allen Arms Hawken shot remarkably well with the round ball; 2-inch groups at 50 yards were the norm. However, I was able to get only 3- and 4-inch groups using Mini-Balls. But this is still more-than-adequate 50- and 100-yard performance for black powder hunting. For the hunter looking for a super-rugged, accurately-styled, late 1840's-period rifle capable of bagging the biggest of big game and able to withstand a lot of punishment, the Allen Arms "Jed Smith" Hawken is indeed a worthwhile choice.

Although the next two mountain rifles are Hawken-like in appearance, they are not referred to as such, much to their manufacturers' credit. ("Too many Hawkens spoil the hunt," I think the old saying goes.) Unlike the Navy and Allen Arms versions, these rifles feature rear sights that are adjustable for elevation via an inset screw. As an added note of interest, both of these next two gunmaking firms were in existence during the black powder era, so they do have history on their side. One of these firms, Lyman, got their start with black powder cartridges in 1878. Today they have taken a welcomed step backwards and now produce an excellent muzzleloader which they call The Great Plains Rifle. It has one of the easiest-to-see front and rear sights of any Hawken I have fired. In contrast to the thick Allen Arms Hawken, the Lyman product has an overall slim feel to its stock, and is therefore easy to carry while on foot. I found the double-set triggers to have a slight bit of roughness and creep, which began to wear off slightly after some use. With its rifle twist of one in 66 inches, the Great Plains Rifle is superbly accurate, a claim attested to by the fact that this rifle won the 1980 Colorado State Hunter's Aggregate Championship. That the folks at Lyman are acutely aware of the hunter's needs is evident, for this is the only Hawken-styled rifle in which *all* of the metalwork is browned, including the nosecap and front sight blade. (I only wish they had changed the brass tip on the ramrod to browned steel, in keeping with the rest of the rifle.) It is also the only Hawken-styled rifle with a coil mainspring. The Great Plains Rifle is available in either flint or percussion, ready-made or kit, and comes in .50 and .54 caliber.

Browning Arms is another name that began receiving recognition during the black powder era. John M. Browning was a prolific inventor, and the firm that bears his name today has produced an extremely well-made hunting rifle dubbed the Jonathan Browning Mountain Rifle. A few desirable design features set this rifle apart from the others: Rather than a double-set trigger, the Browning product features a unique single trigger which may be set by pushing it *forward*. It takes a little getting used to, but it is also much crisper when set than most of the other Hawken-styled rifles; the trigger may be adjusted from 2 pounds to 2 ounces. If you select this gun, you may choose from not two, but three calibers: .45 (for

The Lyman Great Plains Rifle, available in either flintlock or percussion, features a coil mainspring.

small game), .50 (for medium-sized game, such as deer) and, my perennial favorite, the .54 (which the Browning people properly tout for elk, moose, and bear). One of the heaviest hunting rifles made, the approximately 9 pounds of weight of the Mountain Rifle takes up a lot of recoil, even when firing 110-grain loads of FFG, which I found to work best. The reason for the heavier weight of the Browning is the extra attention given to the gun's design. All metal fittings, including the twin barrel wedges, are thick and heavy-duty, although the hammer is stubbier than on most caplocks. Even the wooden ramrod is thicker. A picturesque ram's horn is cast into the bolster, giving the rifle even more character. The cheekpiece on rifles produced up through the first half of 1981 was neither authentic nor very good-looking, and much to Browning's credit, this has been remedied, with all current guns sporting the classic beaver-tail cheekpiece. An excellent booklet on muzzleloading shooting and safety, plus recommended hunting charges, comes with each gun, along with an extra stainless steel nipple. When ordering your Browning Mountain Rifle, be sure to specify the browned version, as a brass-fitted model is made for city dwellers, ne'er-do-wells, and other assorted riffraff.

Leaving the Hawken lode, we next come upon a stylishly designed hunting rifle called the Big Bore Mountain Rifle. It is made by Connecticut Valley Arms, one of the most popular muzzleloading manufacturing firms in the country. To its credit, CVA is another company that has taken the time to create a booklet on black powder shooting and safety that is included with every gun. Although a number of similarly-styled rifles are in CVA's line, the Big Bore is the only one that meets the hunter's criteria. It has a tight, smooth action,

Jonathan Browning Mountain Rifle is a quality hunting arm with two unusual features; the curled rams horn cast onto the bolster, and the unique "set" trigger, which must be pushed *forward* to "set" it for a hair-trigger pull.

[44]

CVA's Big Bore rifle in .58 is the largest caliber single shot made. It is also available in .54 caliber.

browned and blued metalwork, and a rear flat-topped sight which may be adjusted for elevation. The double-set triggers are very crisp for a production gun. Like the Hawken rifles, the CVA Big Bore features two tenons that securely hold the barrel to the stock, and with good reason, for true to its name, the Big Bore comes in your choice of .54 or .58 caliber. No small stuff here; in fact, it is one of the few .58's available in a civilian-styled hunting gun. Its look is that of a classic 1850's sporting rifle. The .58 Big Bore is rifled one turn in 72 inches, but I shoot Minis in it instead, wanting to take advantage of that caliber's extremely potent knockdown power; 110 grains produced over 1,000 foot pounds of energy at 100 yards, and gave me 8-inch groups. You won't snuff out any candle flames with this gun, but whatever gets hit with it will stay down! If you are contemplating going after hard-to-kill game which is normally shot at close range, such as buffalo or moose, consider the CVA Big Bore.

Simplicity in design is perhaps the best way to describe Mowrey's Ethan Allen Rifles. Originally invented in 1837 by the same fellow who created the famous Pepperbox pistol, there were probably less than a hundred such guns ever made. Yet this rifle is as accurate and functional as some of the more popular designs of the 1800's. Today, the muzzleloading hunter can choose from two distinct sizes: the Squirrel Rifle, a small-framed, 7-pound offering available in .36 or .45 caliber (yes, this is the other squirrel gun I mentioned earlier), and the larger 10-pound Plains Rifle in .50 or .54 caliber. For the family that likes to hunt together, the identically-designed Squirrel Rifle and Plains Rifle would seem to make an ideal pair for father and son, husband and wife, big sister and little brother. Like the Ithaca Hawken, the Mowrey rifles are completely handmade in the

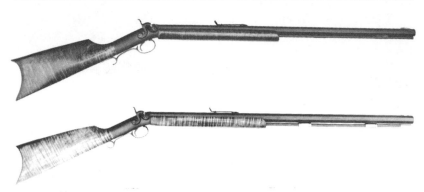

The simple lockwork and design for the Mowrey Ethan Allen Rifle and its big brother companion, the Plains Rifle.

United States, and owner Neil McMullen takes great Texas pride in stating that each of the eight grooves in every barrel is individually cut by hand, one at a time. He also places a unique guarantee on his guns; hunters may obtain free small parts replacements, such as screws and springs, for their guns for the rest of their lives! Of course, it should be mentioned that the Ethan Allen lock only contains five moving parts, making it almost foolproof. It is also satisfyingly accurate with round ball, as any gun should be that is completely made by hand. I was not able to get any noteworthy grouping with conical bullets, however. But the round ball Squirrel Rifle bench-rested cloverleafs with six shots, with cleaning in-between rounds (the smaller calibers foul up faster). The guns come with a small Allen wrench that is used for adjusting both the trigger pull on the rifle and the very deep and wide buckhorn rear sight. One of the most outstanding features of the Mowrey product is the premium grade hand-rubbed curly maple wood used on all of their stocks. Just an extra "plus" from a company that seems to like offering extras. As with the Browning rifle, be sure to specify the browned steel version of Mowrey's fine product, as a brass model is also made. In an effort to please everyone, Neil told me they could "mix and match" any combination of brass and steel parts if a customer so desired, although there may be a slight extra charge. To show he meant business, he placed brass ramrod thimbles on the browned .54 rifle I ordered. I promptly tarnished them with black powder fouling after the photos for this book were taken.

[46]

The firm of Lyman once again enters our camp with their version of the Trade Rifle, a handy halfstock muzzleloader whose best feature is its 28-inch barrel, which is rifled for conical slugs. The gun is reminiscent of the plain but functional hunting rifles carried by early traders of the Far West and northern tributaries. Available in .50 or .54 caliber, the Trade Rifle can be purchased in kit form or ready-made. Either way, you can specify flintlock or percussion; the single trigger is nonadjustable and the lock is powered by a coil spring. The sights are fixed and browned as are the barrel and lock. However, all other metalwork, including the wedge, is brass. The Trade Rifle is a sturdy little gun, but I would replace the brass wedge with a steel one, and would just as quickly tarnish the shiny trigger guard, buttplate, and nosecap.

The next two hunting guns are not for the average black powder sportsman. These are not my thoughts, but come directly from the manufacturers themselves. I know for a fact that these men have personally *turned away* sales because they did not think the customer was ready for their guns! Well, no one ever said muzzleloading manufacturers were not an honest group. Personally, I feel that if a hunter

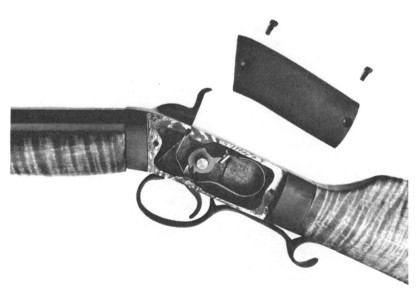

Interior of the Mowrey lock has only five moving parts.

has studied all of the available guns suitable to his sport, and has decided on the one he wants, he should be able to buy it as long as he has the money. Still, you cannot fault the integrity of these two firms, both of which turn out less than 1,000 rifles a year. Even with this comparatively low volume, they have steadfastly refused to sacrifice quality and they strive to improve their products year after year. Their guns certainly deserve a place in this book, and one of their guns should find a place in at least a few racks. I have hunted with both products and I endorse them heartily.

The first of these black powder hunting arms is probably more familiar to most shooters. It is the famous Sharps rifle; in this case

Lyman Trade Rifle is a simply-styled rifle designed to shoot conical bullets. Before taking it hunting, you should dull the brass.

Coil spring of the Lyman Trade Rifle percussion lock.

[48]

The Model 1863 Sporting Rifle, made by Shiloh Sharps, is a carbon copy of the original buffalo gun, and in many ways, it is even better, due to closer machining operations and stronger steel used today.

the well-respected carbon copy made by Shiloh. Actually, the Shiloh Sharps is better than the original, as all parts are interchangeable with other Shiloh guns. Not so with the original mid-1800's product, mainly because its measurements were not as exacting as those in today's guns. The Sharps cannot really be called a true muzzle-loader, because the bullet and charge are loaded from the breech and the old adage "first the powder, then the ball" is reversed. Loading the Sharps is simple: as the lever is swung open, the breech-block slides down, revealing an empty chamber. A pre-greased *conical* bullet is inserted as far forward as it will safely go, 90 to 100 grains of FFG or Pyrodex RS powder fill the cavity, and the breech-block slides up as the lever is closed, effectively sealing off the chamber from any escaping gases. The nipple is then topped off with a musket cap, the hammer cocked and the gun is ready to fire. Because no ramrod is needed, the Shiloh Sharps is the fastest-shooting single-shot rifle available to the hunter today, just as it was the favored rifle of the big game hunters in the last century. Shiloh produces four .54 black powder shoulder guns, but the most ideally suited to the hunter is their Model 1863 Sporting Rifle. Its chambers can easily hold 100 grains of powder (up to 110 grains if poured in carefully), whereas the military models only have a powder capacity of 60 grains, which takes them out of the big game class. Besides the ease of loading, the black powder hunter can make paper cartridges, just as the buffalo hunters did years ago. Shiloh sells a complete paper cartridge-making kit, and it is the classic method of carrying pre-measured charges in the field. The Sharps shooter (no that's not where the word came from!) merely rolls some nitrate-soaked paper around a dowel that is slightly smaller than the rifle chamber. The paper tube is sealed on one end and a pre-measured amount of FFG or Pyrodex RS is poured in. Then the other end of the tube is closed and folded over or glued. That's all there is to it. When the "loaded" paper cartridge is inserted into the Sharps' chamber, it acts as a ramrod and helps seat the bullet. When the breechblock is closed, it slides up and cuts off the back of the sealed paper tube, exposing the powder to the flash hole, which is located right in the middle of the breechblock. It is a very effective system. Some shooters may be familiar with a method of loading the paper tubes with powder, but leaving one end unsealed; this opening is plugged up by inserting the greased slug, so that the entire "cartridge," bullet and powder, goes in at once. However, I prefer to carry paper cartridge and bullet separately, as there is less chance of the greased bullet slipping out of the paper casing, as can sometimes happen during the strenuous activity of a hunt, thereby spilling powder and ball through your possibles bag or pockets. Even tying or gluing the paper to the bullet never seems to work very well. For added precaution, I carry the paper cartridges and greased bullets in the waterproof Butler Creek Quick Loaders, which are discussed in more detail in Chapter Six.

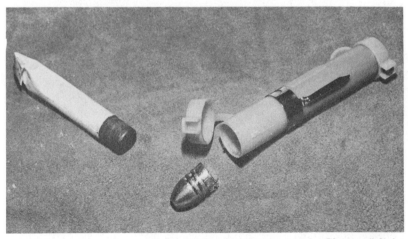

Two methods of carrying powder and bullets for the hunter with a Sharps: *(left)* the traditional one-piece paper cartridge with bullet sealing one end, and *(right)* the Butler Creek Quick Loader with paper-cartridge in "powder" end and pre-greased conical in the "ball" compartment. I prefer the second method.

My custom .54 Gemmer (a Sharps with Hawken-styled wood and browned iron fittings) made by the C. Sharps Arms Company.

There is a close brother to the Shiloh Sharps Company called C. Sharps Arms Company. This firm takes these excellent hunter's rifles and turns them into works of recreated nineteenth century beauty, in the same styles as the original Sharps Rifle Company. This service includes barrels (round, tapered octagon, or half-round in various lengths), stocks (premium to presentation grades in walnut and maple), checkering and engraving. The cost for all this handwork is surprisingly modest, but that is not to imply that these guns are inexpensive. The custom Sharps are among the costliest of all hunting rifles covered in this book, but they certainly add that personalized touch to a gun clearly intended to become a family heirloom.

Another big game muzzleloader to emerge out of the past is the double rifle, a black powder arm made famous by African hunters who wanted the security of more than one shot when pursuing dangerous game on safari. The two barrels and two locks side-by-side was the nineteenth century's answer. Today, Trail Guns Armory has recreated this no-nonsense gun with their Kodiak double rifle. The Kodiak comes .50 caliber side-by-side, .58 side-by-side, and a .50/12-gauge combination, which would make a superb all-purpose gun for the hunter venturing into areas where both feathers and fur were in season. Personally, I prefer the twin-barrel .58 as the ultimate rifle for dangerous game, such as bear, and for hard-to-kill animals, like buffalo, which traditionally require more than one shot to bring down no matter where they are hit. Although the Kodiak shoots well with patched round balls, the one-in-48-inch twist of the bores, plus the intended purpose of this gun really demand that it be shot with conical slugs. However, you will have to do a lot of

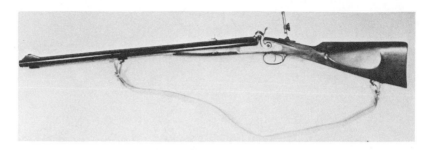

The Kodiak double rifle *(top)*, made by Trail Guns Armory (shown with optional tang sight) is ideal for dangerous game where two quick shots may be needed. However, never cock both hammers at once, as recoil from the first shot could cause the gun to "double" on you and your shoulder! This gun comes with a hooked breech, which makes cleaning easier.

testing to determine which bullet works best. I once went through three pounds of FFG just to finally settle on a workable hunting load that would group the rounds adequately for my .58 double. The .50 caliber seems to group tighter, but I like the harder-hitting advantage of the bigger bullets. Traditionally, double rifles had their barrels "regulated" so that the bullet from each would converge at a specified range, using a single rear sight. Firing at anything in front of or behind that range, and the gun would be off target. TGA has side-stepped this problem by equipping their rifle with *two* Marble folding semi-buckhorn sights, one behind the other. Using the adjusting screws, one sight is calibrated for the right barrel, the other for the left. Although the Kodiak can fire two shots faster than any other muzzleloading rifle, the hunter must take time to flip down one sight and flip up the other. I prefer to zero in with one sight for the right barrel (the one I normally fire first) and then use the same sight for the second barrel, mentally noting where it hits at different ranges. That way I can employ "Kentucky windage" (as discussed in Chapter Five) for what may be a crucial repeat shot without unnecessary loss of time. If you do have that extra few seconds, however, you should employ the second sight to gain additional accuracy. The ruggedness of the Kodiak's construction is exemplified by the fact that the breech-threads are soldered into place. They are never meant to be unscrewed (a difficult feat for a double rifle in the first place. Actually, no rifle should have the breech plug unscrewed, as it can cause excessive wear to the threads, eventually resulting in gas leaks and an unsafe fit. If you *have* to go into the breech, do it from the muzzle.) The Kodiak double rifle is the only gun that comes from the factory with a leather sling, and special Uncle Mike's Hot Shot nipples (see Chapter Six for more information on these features). There is another advantage of the Kodiak for the wilderness hunter; should one lock become inoperable, you still have a rifle you can shoot. The Kodiak is one of the heaviest muzzleloaders made, weighing in at approximately 10 pounds. Part of the reason for the extra weight is a steel-and-spring plunger concealed in the stock to help absorb recoil.

Next in line for the muzzleloading hunter's parade come the military rifles. Taking them in chronological order, the first suitably attired gun for today's hunter is also the first rifled shoulder arm officially adopted by the U.S. government; it is the Model 1803 Harper's Ferry flintlock. The first fifteen of these guns to come off that famed arsenal's assembly line were quickly snatched up by Cap-

Navy Arms 1803 Harper's Ferry is as good a gun today as it was on the Lewis & Clark expedition.

A sturdy workhorse of a hunting rifle, the .58 caliber Model 1841 Mississippi is made by both Dixie and Navy Arms.

tain Meriwether Lewis and "field tested" with honors during the Lewis and Clark expedition. Although originally made in .54 caliber, Navy Arms has enlarged the bore to .58 and today produces a near-perfect replica of that famous rifle. A flintlock with single, nonadjustable trigger, this gun is just as rugged today as its prototype was almost 200 years ago. The large steel rear sight must be filed to bring it on target. Most of the furniture is browned, but the flat brass patchbox should be oxidized before taking this gun out on your own expedition.

From Navy Arms comes the beautiful 1841 Mississippi Rifle, a .58 percussion that achieved undying fame in the hands of Jeff Davis's Mississippi Raiders. The Mississippi Rifle's relatively short 33-inch barrel makes it very fast handling for a military gun, and the sling swivels further add to its versatility. No slings are supplied with any of the military rifles, however, but you can order these from Dixie, Uncle Mike's or Bianchi. Like the Harper's Ferry, the Mississippi sports fixed sights, nonadjustable trigger and (ugh) brass patchbox. A similar rifle is also made by Dixie.

One of my favorite military muzzleloaders for the hunter is the Model 1861 Enfield Muskatoon. Although longer and heavier versions are available (a three-band musket and a two-band model of 1858), the short 24-inch barrel and light 7-pound Musketoon is all the hunter really needs. This .58 caliber "shorty" has extremely accurate adjustable sights and sling swivels. If that were not enough, the Musketoon is the only shoulder arm featuring "progressive rifling," a gradually spiraling twist that helps prevent Minis from stripping out of the rifling when using heavy charges. Of all the military rifles, this is the one I recommend most highly. The Muska-

My favorite military rifle for the hunter is the 1861 Enfield Muskatoon. The .58 shown here is from Euroarms, but similar models are made by Navy Arms, and a more expensive version is being imported from Parker-Hale in England.

toon originally was made in England, and it was used by both sides in the War Between the States. Parker Hale is now reproducing these costly guns, using the original gauges and bone charcoal bluing formula for the "metalwork." Less expensive but equally effective replicas are made by Navy Arms and Euroarms. The Musketoon takes musket caps and Navy Arms sells a handy Parker Hale musket-sized nipple cap, which not only protects the nipple, but helps prevent rain and snow from leaking into your powder charge.

Two other military rifles which achieved popularity during the Great Rebellion and on the American frontier are the Zouave Rifle (made by Dixie Gun Works and Navy Arms) and the Model 1863 Springfield (from Euroarms and Navy). Both rifles are suitable for the hunter, and they represent the highest point of the muzzleloading military-type rifle before the advent of the cartridge arm. These rifles each feature sling swivels, adjustable military sights, and a .58 caliber bore which is rifled for the Mini. The Zouave has a brass patchbox and is also available from Navy Arms in a 20-inch carbine version. The 1863 has brightly polished metalwork which should be dulled or browned before taking it into the field. This particular rifle was extremely popular with hunters of its day, and as a teenager I remember seeing a wooden barrel jammed full of these ex-Union Army rifles in a pawnshop for $10 each!

Next, we come to the "moderns," those muzzleloading rifles designed in this century for this century's shooters. Although a great number of these guns exist, only two are for the hunter. First and foremost in my mind is the American-made Thompson/Center Renegade, one of the most thoroughly thought-out muzzleloading hunting rifles on the market. It is also one of the least expensive, although this in no way should suggest that quality has suffered. Available in

The Thompson/Center Renegade is one of the most thoroughly thought-out modern rifles for the hunter.

By shortening the buttstock, the lightweight Sile Hawken Hunter Carbine would make an ideal rifle for a child.

either .50 or .54 caliber, the Renegade is specifically designed for Maxiballs, but I found it shoots just as well with Minis. A .56 caliber smoothbore is also offered for those hunters in states where rifled black powder arms are not allowed. Both percussion or flintlock actions are available, but the gun really comes into its own with the more reliable caplock. Both locks feature coil springs.

Sturdiness and practicality are the hallmarks of the Renegade. Its buttstock is black steel with a non-slip, non-reflective matte finish. Double-set triggers are fine-tuned just as they come from the factory, exhibiting no creep in the set position. Sights are big, bold, adjustable, and easy to see in even the dimmest twilight. The barrel has a unique tension-retaining spring under the rib to help keep the ramrod from working loose under heavy recoil or on a fast jaunt downhill. The nicely-figured walnut stock is finished in a non-glare oil stain and does not have a nosecap of any kind. The Renegade is strictly a hunting gun, with no frills other than Thompson/Center's standard cast engraved design on the darkly case-hardened lockplate. It is an excellent choice for the primitive hunter who wishes to "go modern." Thompson/Center is another company that has shown they care about the safety of the hunter and the effectiveness of their product by including a rather complete thirty-six page booklet on black powder shooting with each gun. The gun comes with a lifetime warranty.

For the hunter seeking a shorter, lighter version of the modern muzzleloader, I can recommend the Sile Hawken Hunter Carbine. With its 20-inch barrel, it is the shortest and lightest .54 rifle on the market. For that reason alone it would make an ideal child's gun (no one currently makes a version of the once-popular "boy's rifle" and this is probably as close as you will come in a ready-made gun). However, some adjustment of the stock will be necessary in this case. Simply measure the approximate reach from your child's shoulder to his trigger finger/hand position and saw the appropriate amount off of the butt (taking 4 inches off the stock makes the Sile Carbine look more in proportion with its short barrel). Don't throw away that end piece of wood, however; you'll need it to reaffix later as the youngster grows. The Sile Carbine is the only muzzleloading rifle to come with a recoil pad, detachable sling swivels (a good idea in case you do not want them to rattle on the gun when no sling is attached), and a chrome-lined bore, which helps deter rusting (*no* gun is totally immune from the effects of black powder fouling.) Its percussion lock is case-hardened and powered by a coil spring. The barrel is darkly blued, and the brass trigger guard is oxidized to a deep black. The rear sight is adjustable and the bead-and-post front sight is extremely easy to see. Unfortunately, the double-set triggers are a bit rough and should be smoothed up before the full potential of the gun can be achieved. Personally, I do not care much for the checkering on the gun, and wish Sile had left it off, as Thompson/Center did on their Renegade. Nonetheless, the Hunter Carbine does fill a void for the modern muzzleloading hunter.

With the exception of the military rifles, you will notice an absence of patchboxes on all of these top-rated hunting rifles. Ever since the infant years of muzzleloading, gunmakers have been trying to put these useless contraptions in the stocks of rifles. They may add a bit of visual interest to the rifle, but I have never found any practical use for them. They are too small to hold a tuna fish sandwich for lunch and too big to keep the things they are supposed to store, like caps and flint, from rattling and spooking every living thing around you. As for packing along some emergency caps or patches on a hunt, that is why the Good Lord gave us possibles bags and pockets.

All of the Hawken-styled rifles, the "moderns," the Kodiak, the Trade Rifle, and the Big Bore, sport hooked breeches, which means by removing the ramrod and driving out a wedge, the barrel lifts out of the stock for ease of cleaning. The other guns do not have this feature; I do not like to remove the barrels from Kentuckies or military-styled rifles, as over a period of time the areas of the stock where the pins and screws enter become worn and enlarged, often causing a loose fit of the barrel. Instead, percussions may be cleaned by running a tube from the nipple to a bucket of hot, soapy water and "pumping" the fouling out. Any muzzleloader can be cleaned by plugging up the nipple or touch-hole, filling the barrel halfway

Many rifles, such as this Mowrey Plains Rifle, have easy-to-reach clean-out holes for adding powder where there was none before!

with your cleaning solution and swabbing the bore with ramrod and patch. (I usually plug up the bore with my thumb, pick up the gun, slosh everything around and dump the gunk out into the sink when my wife isn't looking.) Do this until the water comes out clean, follow with a few dry patches (the first may come out wet and black, but the rest should gradually become clean and dry) and follow with an oily patch, coating all the lands and grooves of the inside of the bore, as well as the breech area, often overlooked by most shooters. I also unscrew the nipple and clean it thoroughly using cotton swabs to dry out and oil the inside of the bolster and hammer recess of percussion guns. Once a year I will oil the inside of my caplocks, but other than that, I rarely remove the lock from the rifle. Flintlocks, due to the fact that everything goes on outside the gun, must be removed, completely cleaned with a toothbrush in hot soapy water, oiled (a spray is best for getting into all the cracks and crevices), and then replaced after the excess drippy oil is wiped off; you don't want it to leak into the stock and weaken the wood.

For the hunter planning an extended or wilderness adventure, I strongly recommend purchasing an extra lock for your rifle, to take along just for repairs. Though not widely publicized in much of today's literature, this was a common practice of last century's hunters, and one worth resurrecting today. Some firms, such as Dixie and Navy Arms, carry extra locks as part of their standard inventory. Other firms may require you to special order the lock, but either way, it is inexpensive insurance to have along on the hunt.

No black powder arm is 100 percent foolproof, no matter how carefully you load it. Even the best of them occasionally are subject to hangfire. The trigger will be pulled, the hammer will fall and the powder in the pan or cap on the nipple will go off . . . but not the gun. *Do not* immediately reload. Sometimes a faint spark will still be smoldering in the breech and, suddenly, with no warning, the gun will fire after a few seconds. For the hunter whose muzzle was aimed at a nice, fat buck, these can be especially trying times, as you do not want to lose your trophy. But then again, you do not want to lose your hand by sending your hunting charge through it as you are reloading. The best practice, if possible, is to continue holding the gun on your quarry for a few seconds, just in case your rifle decides to finally go off. If nothing happens, keep the muzzle pointing away from anything you don't want to shoot, and immediately recap or prime. If your buck is still within range, take aim and fire again. If your gun remains silent, you are going to have to call it a missed shot. Say farewell to the buck, kick your hunting partner in the shin, and then sit down with your rifle. Remove the priming or pluck off the cap and unscrew the nipple, and probe around the flash channel into the breech with a vent pick or thin wire to ascertain that there is powder in the back of the bore. Sometimes we get a little excited and ram the ball down first, in which case you will have to pull it out with a corkscrew-type "worm" threaded onto your ramrod, or shoot the ball out by trickling some powder into the breech through the flash-hole or clean-out opening. Be sure the ball is seated against the charge, however, or you will blow out a bulge in your barrel and maybe yourself. However, assuming that you have maintained your senses and really did pour powder down the bore first, the next thing to do is to get some new powder into the main charge by either pushing it into the flash-hole of a flintlock or filling up the flash-hole and nipple of a percussion gun. As in loading for the first time, you may want to gently slap the side of your upright rifle to make sure the powder charge has settled into the breech and flash-hole areas. I also make it a point to give the ball a couple of light taps with the ramrod just to make sure everything is seated properly. Then, with a new priming charge or a fresh cap, continue your hunt. Chances are the next time you see Mr. Venison, your rifle will speak loudly.

I once had the interesting experience of carrying a Kodiak double rifle for two hours in a blinding blizzard, following an ice-laced stream back to my car. (If you are starting to think most of my big game hunting has been in lousy weather, think how *I* must feel!) In true bad-weather style, I was carrying the Kodiak slung over my shoulder with the muzzles facing down. As I crested what I thought was a steep hill, it suddenly turned out to be a deep snowdrift; the frozen crust broke and I plunged through, feet and gun muzzle first, totally immersing myself in the cold, white fluff. By the time I made it back to the car and poured a cup of hot coffee from my thermos, the snow in the gun had melted, soaking the powder charges in both barrels. I unscrewed the nipples, dug some of the packed, wet powder out with a paper clip, filled them with fresh FFG and, after clearing out the debris from the bores, successfully fired both barrels into

a dead tree. It sure beats trying to yank the charge with a ball-puller, a dubious practice at best.

Armed with a top quality black powder hunting rifle, and the knowledge of how to use it, there is virtually no challenge the muzzleloading hunter cannot meet, if his mind and body are strong. That is the legacy we have inherited. That is also the future history we forge each time we enter the wilderness with our most treasured possession, the black powder hunting rifle.

CHAPTER THREE

THE RENAISSANCE OF BLACK POWDER SHOTGUNNING

B ack in the early 1950's, when I first became infatuated with hunting winged and furry game with a muzzleloading shotgun, I had to make do with what was available at the time. There were no replica guns in those days. Instead, my black powder scattergunning activities were accomplished by loading 75 grains of FFG black powder and a handful of Arizona dry wash pebbles (no one sold lead shot in my neighborhood and I could not have afforded it even if they did) down the shot-out barrel of an old 1863 Trenton Civil War musket I had picked up in a pawn shop for $15. I kept everything packed in that old Union Army tube by ramming down wadding made from pieces of the Republic and Gazette newspaper. That makeshift shotgun must have patterned like a pinball machine, but in spite of it all, occasionally I managed to bag a few doves and rabbits in the dry washes of the Salt River Valley. For me, those were lean but fun-filled and formative years, as I gradually became acquainted with the centuries-old art of black powder scattergunning.

Practical muzzleloading shotguns have been with us since the 1750's, when they were first handcrafted by English gunsmiths. However, it wasn't until one hundred years later—appropriately enough, during the Victorian era—that they reached their pinnacle of perfection, as far as design and performance were concerned. During that time, bird and small game hunting with muzzleloading scatterguns enjoyed an undisputed surge of popularity for both survival and recreation; its early aficionados included mountain men such as Carson and Bridger and immigrant families heading west. Later, devotees of the front-loading shotgun included the western rancher, the farmer of the Midwest, and the cravated businessman of the East, as well as sportsmen throughout the world, all of whom appreciated the muzzleloader's beauty, handling, and game-getting performance. Unfortunately, all this had come to an end by the 1880's when the fixed-shell breechloading shotgun was finally accepted by hunters.

It took over a hundred years for the muzzleloading shotgun to

John D. Baird, editor of *The Buckskin Report*, proves his expertise by bagging hard-to-hunt chukars with an original Westley Richards 1854 percussion double.

regain its rightful place in the shooting sports. Even though the "re-birth" of muzzleloading is generally acknowledged to have started in 1954, the scattergun has, until recently, lagged behind its rifled brethren in popularity. The reasons for this unfortunate situation were that there was a scarcity of safe, shootable, and affordable shotguns, and a lack of readily-available shooting paraphernalia required by the front-loaders. There also was the inconvenience of carrying all this equipment into the field, plus the mistaken belief that the muzzleloading shotgun was not as effective as its modern, fixed-shell counterpart.

Today, all these negative notions have evaporated like a cloud of FFG smoke in an autumn wind, thanks to two important factors. The first is the growing number of hunters discovering the fun, effectiveness, and economy of muzzleloading. Shot for shot, it costs less to shoot a muzzleloader than it does "store bought" ammunition. And for convenience, a front-loaded shotgun charge is fairly well expended after 60 yards, making it ideal for hunting in areas which otherwise might be considered too densely populated for safe shooting.

The second impetus to the front-loading shotgunner's resurgence is the increased number of manufacturers who have entered the black powder hunter's camp. As a result, an amazing variety of products has come out in recent years. Some are carry-overs of original equipment our great-grandfathers might have used; others are new and innovative creations designed to make the black powder shotgunner's sport more enjoyable than at any other time in history. Indeed, muzzleloading shotgunning has come full circle since those pre-replica days when I first became interested in the sport. But even back then, when replicas were non-existent and originals normally sold for give-away prices by today's standards, good quality muzzleloading shotguns in safe, shootable condition were hard to come by. Fortunately for black powder hunters today, that situation has entirely changed. Readers of this book can choose from some of the finest replica guns that equal and even surpass the best quality shotguns of the nineteenth century. Thanks to the dedicated efforts of a few manufacturers and importers, the twentieth century black powder shotgunner has a choice of single- or double-barreled scatterguns, most patterned after original 1840–70 era arms.

Black powder sportsmen of the past had the mixed blessing of being able to select from a confusing array of gauges ranging from the mammoth 1-gauge all the way down to the 14. Today's shotgunner will find his gun-selecting task made easier, as only two of the most popular gauges of the past are available in replica smoothbores: the 12- and the 10-gauge. Each has its place on the hunting scene and we will look into the merits of both.

In spite of what you may read in well-intentioned advertising literature, the fact is that every replica muzzleloading shotgun on today's market comes with improved cylinder-bored choke, for throwing the widest possible pattern. However, as we shall learn in the next few pages, it is possible to vary your loading techniques to produce patterns as tight as a 50 percent modified. This ability to load to your own specifications is just one of the many advantages of muzzleloading shotgunning.

Gauges and chokes aside, my personal preference is the traditional side-by-side double, even though very little of my furred or feathered game has ever been taken with that second barrel. But for me, it is psychologically reassuring to have that extra tube loaded and ready, should I ever need it; and on a few occasions, I actually *have* scored with the second barrel after missing with the first. All this notwithstanding, I just happen to *like* the way a good double looks and feels in my hands.

In the twin tube category, I feel best values for the money are two classically-styled 12-gauges, the Dixie Gun Works Double and the Navy Arms Deluxe Upland Double. Both guns are available in kit form if you have some extra time on your hands and want to save a few dollars. However, I should mention that the factory-assembled guns are very well made and for the small difference in price, I per-

The Navy Arms classic side-by-side double 12 gauge.

Euroarms 12-gauge, single-barreled Magnum Cape Gun.

Dixie Gun Works' hard-hitting 10-gauge double. A similar gun is produced by Trail Guns Armory.

sonally would rather purchase a completed shotgun and spend my extra time shooting it. Both makes of scatterguns sport 28-inch tubes, have European walnut stocks with hand-checkering, and feature stamped or cast engraving on lock, hammers and trigger guard.

For those duck and goose hunters wanting to put a little more power and range in their offshore and marshland shooting activities (or who simply want to get better patterns from their milder 12-gauge loads), there are also two very well-made 10-gauge doubles produced by Trail Guns Armory and Dixie Gun Works. Both guns are nearly identical; it just depends on whose name you want on the barrel. Unlike the 12-gauge muzzleloading doubles on today's market, these large-bore scatterguns feature long 30¾-inch, beautifully browned barrels, a cheek piece on the left side of the stock, twin bead front and middle sights, and sling swivels. The Trail Guns Armory percussion weighs in at a hefty 9 pounds thanks to a spring-pistoned weight concealed in the stock to help absorb recoil. The Dixie double does not have this feature and as a result, is about 1½ pounds lighter. On both guns, ornate Victorian-era engraving adorns all metal parts with the exception of the richly-browned barrels. For those hunters who already own a Trail Guns Armory double rifle, as described in Chapter Two, a separate set of 12-gauge shotgun barrels can be purchased from TGA that will fit their Kodiak, thus giving them two guns in one.

Shotgunners preferring the lighter weight and ease of pointability of a single-barreled scattergun have a limited number to choose from, and all are available only in 12 gauge. (Although there are a number of well-made muzzleloading single-barreled shotguns on the market, many feature brass receivers, or furniture, which I consider unsuitable for hunting due to the reflective qualities of that metal.) One of the best single-shots I have hunted with is the Magnum Cape Gun, imported by Euroarms of America. This 12-gauge copy of an 1850-style English sporting fowler has a 32-inch barrel with a clean-out screw on the left side of the breech — a handy feature that not only makes it easy to remove caked-up fouling or moist powder that can accumulate under the flash-hole of the nipple, but also enables an overly enthusiastic shooter to trickle in a few grains of black powder in the event he neglected to do so prior to ramming his shot and wad firmly into the breech, a situation known to occur during the excitement of the hunt. The Cape Gun also features a nicely-finished, hand-checkered walnut stock. Light, tasteful engraving accents the hammer, triggerguard, and lockplate, which is polished to a dull, silver matte sheen. All other metal parts are blued, making the gun an extremely attractive representation of an 1850's European-styled caplock for the gentleman hunter.

Another well-made single-barreled scattergun suitable for the black powder sportsman is the browned steel version of Mowrey Gun Works Ethan Allen Shotgun. Using the same, simple 1837-style action and design of their functional rifles (see Chapter Two) this 12-gauge percussion features a 32-inch octagonal barrel, single brass bead front sight, and like the Euroarms Cape Gun, has a handy clean-out screw located near the breech. It is the only shotgun featuring an adjustable trigger, and it comes with beautiful curly maple stocks as *standard* equipment. The Mowrey product is the only scattergun that does not have the easy-to-clean hooked breech feature. However, unlike the other replica shotguns we have discussed, the Mowrey arm is the only one made in the United States; all the others are manufactured in Italy, although it should be noted that every shotgun mentioned is of top quality.

By now you have probably noted the lack of any flintlock shotguns in this chapter. That's because there aren't any, at least not for sale on the mass market. Of course, you can always get one created for you by some of the custom black powder gunsmiths. However, even if there were so paradoxical a firearm as a flintlock scattergun, chances are it would not meet the requirements of the black powder hunter. That is because of the very mechanism of the firelock itself, in which the priming charge is exposed to the wind, rain and moisture most waterfowlers and some upland hunters must endure in the pursuit of their game. It is bad enough, when hunting with a flintlock rifle, to have your carefully poured FFFFG priming charge whisked away by the wind, or to sit on a stand and watch the rivulets of rainwater quietly trickling into your flashpan. But in the sometimes fast and furious snap shooting that shotgunning demands, it is totally exasperating to hear the flint strike the frizzen, and have nothing happen. Some of the foul weather techniques listed in Chapter Eight may work for the first shot of the day, but after that, it is usually over for the moisture-laden flintlocker who wants to bag an-

Practically all current muzzleloading shotguns feature the convenient hooked breech for easy take-down, with doubles sporting twin hooks.

other rabbit for the pot or who sees a second flock circling his blind. In addition, for wing shooting, when the flinter is pointed up at an angle, the priming charge will often drift back, away from the touchhole. It may ignite with a reassuring "whoof," but the charge in your barrel will remain silent. Indeed, the best thing that ever happened for flintlock shotgunning was the invention of the percussion cap.

I once had occasion to fire a custom-made flintlock double in the honest but mistaken notion of both the maker and myself that I might buy it. That shooting experience can best be described as memorable. Firing the right barrel was satisfactory, as the gun had a finely-tuned fast-action lock. But when the left barrel was touched off, there was something quite unforgettable about having the outside priming charge burst forth so close to one's face, leaving a smoldering reminder of that particular shot on your eyebrows, cheek, and the brim of your hat, should you still be in possession of all three items after the shot is fired.

However, for those of you who are masochistic enough to want to try your hand at flintlock scattergunning or if you are honestly tired of bagging your limit each season and want to put a new challenge into an old sport, the best bet on today's market is to pick up one of the finer quality Brown Bess replica muskets from either Navy Arms or Dixie Gun Works. A word of caution: Watch out for the cheaper Japanese-made replicas; they look good, but will not hold up as well for the hunter as the better grade guns offered by these two firms.

The Brown Bess is an exact replica of the Second Model used by both the British and the Colonists during the American Revolution and its 41¾-inch long smoothbore is approximately .75 caliber, which translates into 12 gauge. If you feel that this full-stocked military musket is a mite too much to swing at a high-flying teal, then I recommend you check out the "carbine" version of the Brown Bess offered by Allen Arms, which sports a 30-inch smoothbore barrel and is called the Trade Musket. With the exception of the barrel length and a "spirit dragon" etched on the brass sideplate, this gun is identical to its big brother in design and quality. But no matter which of the Brown Bess muskets you decide upon, be prepared to do a lot of pre-season experimentation with it. The long throw of the military lock and hammer takes some getting used to and patterning

Shotgunning with a flintlock takes a lot of practice and perseverance. I hunted all day to bag this lone pheasant with my Allen Arms trade musket.

a smoothbore musket that was originally designed for troops using the round ball can be a real challenge. I once took the Allen Arms Trade Musket out on an all-day pheasant hunt, just to see for myself what it could do. The results of that day's activity are pictured in this chapter (no, there aren't any more birds hidden under my shirt; that lone cock was *it*, and I'm convinced I just got lucky).

With the exception of the Trail Guns Armory double, all of the above-mentioned scatterguns weigh in at a scant 6 to 7½ pounds. In my humble, abject, and non-arguable opinion, this is much too light for any kind of enjoyable shooting. The fault lies not with the manufacturers, but with Nature herself. Unfortunately, thanks to the growing demands of our society, there is a scarcity of close-grained, high-density (i.e., heavy) wood. As a result, more and more firearms firms are turning out lighter guns, which does little towards dampening recoil. In spite of its growing acceptance in this country, I have never felt that lightness belongs in beer, bourbon, or guns. While the first two items may be open to discussion, the third one definitely is not. Granted, a 6½-pound muzzleloader is easier to carry all day than an 8-pounder, but when that all-important shot is fired, the heavier gun wins out, especially in shotgunning. The black powder big game hunter rarely has the problem of recoil to worry about, even though he may be shooting bone-breaking loads; chances are he will not touch off more than one or two shots at his quarry all season. But the black powder shotgunner has the opportunity to expend twenty or more FFG charges in a single day, if he has the good fortune to be stationed in a productive blind or in a heavily inhabited cornfield. As a result, many hunters have trouble shouldering their scatterguns after a few muscle-pounding shots. And with good reason.

When firing black powder hunting loads of approximately three drams of FFG (equivalent to 82 grains of black powder), you are creating a tremendous amount of pressure, inertia, and "felt" recoil. Exactly how much is "felt" is easy to determine, and you don't need much sophisticated equipment to do it. I have perfected a fairly reliable method for recoil measurement that has been successfully employed over the years. It is known as the Hacker Blue-Shoulder Technique (HBST). Using this system, one merely test-fires a num-

Ignition, velocity, and gas dispersion were all improved greatly by installing Hot Shot nipples on shotguns.

ber of black powder loads on a given day, and the next morning, he visually inspects his right shoulder (naturally, this technique should be reversed for southpaws). Judging by the degree of discoloration on the shoulder, the extent of recoil received by a black powder shotgun can be dramatically gauged (no pun intended). For example, a light blue-green shoulder would indicate a light, upland load. A medium blue is a standard, all-around load, which only becomes noticeably uncomfortable at the end of a day's hunt. A deep purple-blue is unfortunately the most common with the heavy-duty loads most of us are forced to shoot in today's lightweight muzzleloading shotguns.

One obvious solution to help diminish recoil is to wear heavier clothing. This is fine for late fall and winter forays, even though body movement is hampered to a degree. But much bird hunting is done in the warm days of early fall, not to mention small game hunting in the spring. This mild weather hunting tends to turn the heavily-clad sportsman into a walking sauna, and bulky clothing can become more of a hindrance than a help. Adding a recoil pad to a muzzleloading shotgun is another solution to the problem, but to my purist mind, is akin to putting a scope on a caplock rifle; if you want to "go modern," then get one of those "new" self-contained cartridge shotguns. For the black powder fraternity, much of the satisfaction lies in shooting a scattergun that *looks* like it came out of the past. Thus, the problem remains: what to do about recoil? Fortunately for today's shooters, there *is* a remedy. It is called the Edwards Recoil Reducer.

Invented by Jesse Edwards, this recoil reducer has been around for quite a while, although Jesse told me its benefits were never publicly applied to muzzleloaders until I decided to give it a try. Basically, the reducer consists of a patented spring-loaded metal tube that is inserted into a hole drilled in the wooden buttstock of a shoulder arm. The hole is then concealed by the gun's buttplate — ideal for muzzleloading shotguns. Jesse's anti-recoil principle is based on Newton's Third Law of Motion: For every force forward, there is an equal force expended in the opposite direction. When I decided to put his recoil reducers through a test, I discovered Edwards' service is unbelievably fast. I shipped the stock portion of my Dixie Double 12-gauge shotgun to Edwards via U.P.S. on Monday. That Friday, the gun was delivered to my house with not one, but two reducers installed. (Jesse promises same-day service, but in this case, he must have had his workshop in the back of a delivery truck en route to my home!) The end result? The Jesse Edwards product reduced my black powder shotgun recoil by 40 percent. And according to my blue shoulder test, after spending a half day test-firing loads of 3½ drams of FFG backing a 1½ ounce charge of shot, there was absolutely no shoulder discoloration. The Dixie Double I was using was not only a lot more enjoyable to shoot, but the added 12 ounces in the stock caused by the two recoil reducers actually improved the gun's balance, shifting it over the locks and increasing its pointability. If you prefer shooting heavy, feather-penetrating hunting loads out of today's muzzleloading shotguns, I strongly recommend that you send the breech and stock portion of your gun (or

You don't always need two barrels to be successful. I bagged a table-full of pheasant with this single-barreled Magnum Cape Gun.

if you have a Mowrey product, just send the whole gun, as removing the stock might damage that beautiful wood) to Jesse Edwards at the address given in Chapter Ten. You may want to write first and get his latest cost of installation, as prices have been known to vary. Get prices for both one and two reducers so you can make a realistic decision based upon recoil and money. Personally, I opt for the double mode, as I don't feel there is such a thing as too *little* recoil. If you order now, with Jesse's fast service, you'll probably have your charcoal burner back in plenty of time for the hunting season; maybe even before you finish this chapter.

Another relatively new product which isn't always associated with black powder scatterguns in the much heralded Uncle Mike's stainless steel Hot Shot nipples. Prior to this invention, percussion shotgun shooters using a double gun would often get a cheek full of hot gases and semi-charred hands when firing the lock closest to their face. It is somewhat akin to a right-handed shooter firing a left-handed gun. But the new Uncle Mike's Hot Shot nipples have eliminated part of that problem; they effectively dispel the gases. Another bonus is that the nipples, when installed on any black powder shotgun, will prevent those high inner-breech pressures from blowing your hammer back to half-cock after each shot, a sear-wrenching experience at best. I also found that the nipples increase velocity slightly — usually 3 to 5 percent — so after installation, you may find you'll be using less powder in your favorite load to achieve the same pattern. And of course, the stainless steel construction insures that the nipples will last as long as your gun. The Hot Shot nipples are available at most gun stores and are an inexpensive and worthwhile investment for the muzzleloader who wants to get the maximum enjoyment and performance out of his black powder shotgun. Take your old nipple with you, so that you will be sure of obtaining the correct screw thread (the Hot Shot nipples come in a variety of sizes to fit most U.S. and imported guns).

In conversations with other scattergunners (muzzleloading and otherwise), I am always surprised to learn that the practice of patterning a shotgun is rapidly becoming a lost art. A shotgunner's failure to pattern his gun is tantamount to a big game hunter not zeroing in his rifle prior to a hunt. But evidently, in the mind of the shotgunner, there is a mistaken notion that because he is blasting forth with a cloud containing hundreds of pellets, no quarry is safe from its lethal effect. Absolutely false! I've seen shotgun patterns that were so open a flock of geese could fly through them sideways, without ruffling their down. Conversely, these same shotguns, worked up (or down) to the proper load, have been made to pattern so tightly that even an anemic snake would be assured of getting a deadly dose of pellet poisoning. The secret is in shotgun patterning, and muzzleloaders have the distinct advantage of being able to tailor-make their loads in the field and after every shot to achieve maximum effectiveness, depending on terrain, range and weather. It's simply a matter of finding the best combination of black powder, or Pyrodex, and shot that is right for your particular gun. And make no mistake about it; although mass-produced on modern ma-

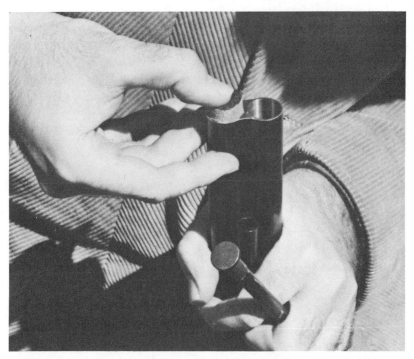

Thick cork over-powder wads must be firmly and carefully forced into muzzle, to keep from splitting. Soaking them in a solvent, such as Hodgdon's Spit Patch or CVA's Grease Patch can ease this loading chore and help keep your smoothbore relatively free from fouling.

[79]

chinery, each muzzleloading shotgun *will* shoot differently. It's up to all of us, as responsible and effective hunters, to find out how differently. To do that, it is necessary to acquaint ourselves with the correct way to load our black powder scattergun, and then how to pattern it.

It should be pointed out that loading a muzzleloading shotgun takes more time than loading a muzzleloading rifle. First (after cleaning out all oil from the empty barrel and chambers and making sure that your nipple vent is clear by popping a cap or two on it), a measured powder charge is poured down the barrel. Then a thick cork or cardboard over-powder wad is *firmly* rammed home. On top of that is poured the measured charge of shot. This is kept in place by a thin cardboard over-shot wad, which is *firmly* rammed down upon the shot. Then the nipple is capped and you are ready to go. I should mention that, as far as I know, the only available source for U.S. shooters to obtain ready-made over-shot and over-powder wads is from Dixie Gun Works. Of course, you can always pre-cut your own wads from sheet cork and shirt cardboard as I did for many years, but I have found the "store-bought" wads to be both economical and convenient, and nowadays, they are all I use.

Black powder shotgun loads must be *firmly* rammed down with the same amount of pressure for each shot, to insure consistency of pattern.

A commonly-asked question for which there is no definite answer is, "How much powder and shot should I use for a good hunting load?" The answer, of course, depends upon the type of gun you have, what you will be hunting with it, and the individual characteristics of both you and your firestick. Normally, the rule of the old-timers was to load an equal amount of powder and shot. It should be remembered that, unlike the rifled muzzleloader in which powder charges are measured in grains, shotgun charges are calibrated in drams. To ease the confusion, one dram equals about 27½ grains of black powder, or the same volume of Pyrodex (remember, Pyrodex is measured by *volume*, not weight, which makes it easy to use with your black powder measure). For your reference, here is a rather standard nineteenth-century table I have prepared, showing shot ounces compared with equal volumes of powder, given in both drams and grains:

Ounces of Shot	Drams of Powder	FFG Powder Equivalent in Grains
1	2½	68
1⅛	2¾	75
1¼	3	82
1⅜	3¼	89
1½	3½	96
1⅝	3¾	102
1¾	4	109
1⅞	4¼	116
2	4½	124
2⅛	4¾	131
2¼	5	138

Normally, you will achieve your best patterns with the 12-gauge gun by going no higher than 3½ drams of powder and 1½ ounces of shot. Sometimes your best shooting will be done with considerably less powder. For example, when patterning the European Cape Gun for a *Guns & Ammo* Field Test a few years ago, I found excellent patterns were obtained with only 3 drams of FFG powder and 1½ ounces of No. 6 shot. This mild, slightly shot-heavy load enabled me to drop four out of five pheasants one October afternoon. My

12-gauge double, however, takes 3½ drams and 1½ ounces of shot nicely. The big 10-gauge can handle 4 drams with ease, pushing loads of 1½ to 2 ounces of shot into some nice improved cylinder and even modified patterns. I have yet to find justification to load these big bore goose guns over 4 drams — the guns can take it, but chances are your shoulder can't. They *do* kick! Besides, in muzzleloading shotgunning, I have found that too much powder will literally blow your pattern open, causing the shot to spread. Conversely, too little powder will result in a loss of velocity and range. Therefore, practice and consistency are the answers to the powder-and-shot question: find the best combination for your gun and stick to it.

As we have previously noticed, most of today's well-made muzzleloading shotguns are open bored. That means they will have a fairly wide choke, usually conducive to close-range (from 25 to 30 yards) upland shooting. For tighter patterns and longer ranges (up to 40 yards with the 12-gauge and as far out as 50 yards with the big 10), plastic shot cups can be used over the powder. Now I realize some brain-tanned front-stuffers out there may cringe at the thought of ramming so vile a substance as plastic down the barrel of their muzzleloader. But I consider muzzleloading to be one of the most relaxing sports known to modern man (there's an analogy for you!), and anything that helps me obtain greater enjoyment (i.e., convenience and effectiveness) from that sport is not only permissible, but is a downright necessity. Shot cups and gauges notwithstanding, for practical and humane purposes, I have always considered 40 yards to be the maximum practical range for any black powder shotgun. Farther out, the pellets disperse too widely and lose too much power for consistently clean kills. Yes, there is always the campfire tale of the buckskinner who managed to drop a high-flying teal at sixty yards with a single 12-gauge shot fired from the hip, but these stories are the exception, not the rule. The black powder hunter who wants to bring game home for the table waits until his target is within the proven killing range of his gun before shooting. And the only way to determine the best range and load for your gun is to pattern it.

Patterning a muzzleloading shotgun is not only necessary, it is simple...and fun! All you need is a 4 × 4 foot sheet of butcher paper

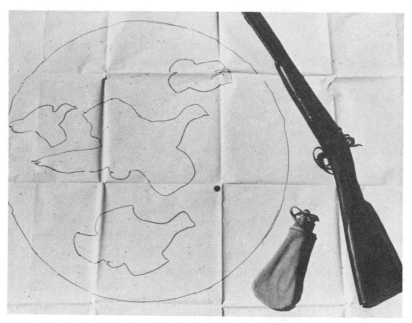

A graphic illustration of why every shotgunner should work up good patterns before taking his scattergun out to the field or marsh. This pattern within the 30-inch circle was fired at 40 yards with 3½ drams of FFG in back of 1½ ounces of No. 6 shot. As you can see, pheasant outline (which is also approximately the size of a duck) is in the killing zone. Dove *(left)* could conceivably fly through the shot pattern. Quail *(bottom)* is as good as on the table. So is the grouse *(top)*, but if he was flying a little higher or faster (as they usually do), he could be "the one that got away." Oh yes, that heavy dot in front of the pheasant was the point of aim!

tacked onto a board. Mark the center of this "target" with a black or orange dot, to be used as an aiming point. From a distance of 40 yards, benchrest your shotgun, aim for the center of the paper and fire your charge. Using a cardboard template cut in a 30-inch diameter circle, cover the largest concentration of your shot on the target. Then trace the circumference of the circle onto your patterning paper. By evaluating the location of the circle in relationship to your aiming point, you can tell just where your shotgun is shooting. (Contrary to popular belief, most of today's muzzleloading shotguns do not shoot directly to point-of-aim. Once you realize this fact, you are well on your way to bagging more game with fewer shots.) Next comes the trial-and-error method of varying your powder and shot combination to produce the densest loads for your gun. The importance of this procedure becomes even more apparent if you will cut out life-size templates of the game you are planning to hunt (i.e., running rabbit, flying duck, etc.) and place these within your shot pattern. In this way, you can tell just how many pellets will strike your quarry in the "killing zone"—which does *not* include ear, tail and wing hits. I consider five 'killing zone" hits to be the absolute minimum for effective and humane shotgun hunting. Anything more than that and you're ready to leave the patterning board and take to the field!

Generally speaking, I've found my best hunting loads fall in the 2½- to 3½-dram vicinity, behind a 1- to 1½-ounce charge of shot. The question of what size of shot to use always comes up, so I have included this chart to help you make a decision. Frankly, there are thirteen basic shot sizes on today's market, ranging from the pebble-size No. 9 all the way up to the .36 caliber oo buckshot. My experience has been that it takes too much money and storage space to keep more than a few shot sizes around the house, so I do all of my scattergunning with two basic sizes, using No. 6's for upland birds and small game, and loading up with No. 4's for turkey and duck. This has worked extremely well for me in all of today's replica smoothbores, although you may want to refine your shot selection even further to fit your own shooting whims. That's part of the fun of front-stuffing your smoothbore!

Recommended Shot-To-Game Chart
(for 12- and 10-gauge muzzleloaders only)

Shot Size	Game
No. 2, No. 4	Goose, Turkey
No. 4, No. 6	Duck, Rabbit, Squirrel
No. 6	Pheasants, Grouse (also suitable for head shots on Turkey)
No. 6, No. 7½	Dove, Quail, Woodcock, Snipe

Although knowledgeable muzzleloading hunters do not have to be told, there might be one or two "pilgrims" out there who want to experiment with life and limb, so I will state the obvious: for shot-gunning, *always use FFG or Pyrodex RS—never* smokeless powder. The guns can't take it and consequently, neither can you. And

speaking of powder, I find that in the 12-gauge, either FFG or Pyrodex RS works equally well. However, in the bigger 10-gauge
smoothbore, especially when shooting heavier loads in the 3½- to 4-
dram category, I usually use just Pyrodex, as these high-octane
charges tend to produce more fouling, which is not quite as severe
with the replica black powder as it is with the nitrate-charcoal-sulfur
stuff.

To compute the type of choke you are obtaining when patterning your shotgun (not necessary to know, but fun to do — and it
makes you a more knowledgeable hunter), just count up the number of pellet holes that hit within your 30-inch circle and divide that
number by the number of shot contained in the load you are shooting. To make life easier, here is an appropriate shot count, per the
four sizes listed in the chart above:

Shot Size	Approximate Number of Shot in Ounces						
	1	1⅛	1¼	1½	1⅝	1⅞	2
2	87	98	109	131	141	163	174
4	135	152	168	203	220	253	270
6	225	253	281	338	368	424	450
7½	350	398	439	525	569	656	700

Thus, if you are shooting 1½ ounces of No. 6 shot, and you
count up 114 within your 30-inch circle, that means 114 ÷ 338 = 34
percent, which is a cylinder choke. Here's how the choke percent-
ages break down: 30–35 percent = cylinder (the most common choke
for muzzleloaders); 36–45 percent = improved cylinder (possible to
obtain by working up your load carefully); 46–55 percent = modified (this is the tightest I've ever been able to pattern any black powder shotgun — maybe you can do better); 65 percent on up = full
choke.

When patterning your scattergun, it is wise to always wear
shooting glasses and ear protection. When shooting those doubles,
I also make it a practice to wear a long-sleeve shirt and gloves, at
least on the hand supporting the barrel, especially when approaching loads of 3½ drams or more. Those hot gases on the left-hand
side of the gun can smart!

All the items needed for a successful day of shotgunning: pre-measured charges, pre-greased overshot and over-powder wads (kept in plastic bag to keep grease from contaminating everything), and shot pouch. Note Uncle Mike's Palm Saver and Dixie Gun Works' Model 1817 pistol ramrod which I use to start thick wads down the bore.

Once you know where your shotgun is shooting and have your hunting load established, you're ready to take to the field. However, therein lies another situation that has been a stumbling block for shooters up until recently — in-the-field reloading. This is not because it is difficult, but due to the fact that your shotgun requires a variety of paraphernalia. The scattergun hunter must carry percussion caps, powder, over-powder wads, shot, and over-shot wads, not to mention nipple pick and nipple wrench for emergencies, and, of course, a game bag for both the sure-shots and the optimists! Happily, with the exception of the game bag, all of these elements can easily be transported by one of two methods, with room left over for a noontime snack.

The first method is the proverbial bush coat, a longtime favorite of mine. (The bush coat's use for riflemen is discussed in Chapter

The Dixie Gun Works Civil War Haversack is ideal for hunting upland game.

Seven.) With its many accordioned pockets, this coat can carry every item a shotgunner might need. All that remains is for the hunter to decide which pockets will carry what, so that with a little practice he can reach instantly for the desired item without a moment's hesitation.

For those shooters who don't like bush coats, there is another option, the haversack. (Most Mountain Man "possibles bags" are normally too small to carry every shotgunning item needed.) Dixie Gun Works sells a Civil War Haversack which is an exact copy of the canvas, over-the-shoulder carrying pouch used by both sides in the War Between the States. It also makes an excellent, rugged and inexpensive shotgunner's bag. This one, sturdy item with its button-down flap will hold everything listed above. You might even consider obtaining an extra haversack to use as a game bag. For an added touch of realism, you might do as I did and replace those plastic buttons with either the pewter or "CSA" variety, both of which are also sold by Dixie.

Fast reflexes, a good dog, and a trusted back-up buddy made this a perfect hunt. I shot this pheasant, using a black powder L. C. Smith double.

As long as we are on the subject of shotgunning paraphernalia sold by Dixie, I would like to make note of two products obtainable from those folks which have not been available to us charcoal-burners for many moons. The first, and to my mind the most needed item, is real-life, honest-to-goodness over-powder and over-shot wads in both 10 and 12 gauge. Ever since the world turned to plastic shot cups and shells, these two seemingly simple components have been harder to find than purple ducks. But Dixie has them and I would advise any serious muzzleloading shotgunner to stock up on a season's supply. The other item which is a "must" for in-the-field shooting is Dixie's Irish or English style leather shot pouch, which I much prefer over the copper or brass variety as it does not make as much noise in the field and will not reflect sunlight. For my hunting, I use the Irish pouch, which features a pre-measured "scoop" that can be set for 1, 1¼, or 1½ ounces of shot. The pouch itself holds enough chilled shot for approximately twenty loadings, just about right for a day's shooting.

For safety reasons as well as weight, I dislike carrying large amounts of powder with me in the field. Therefore, I always opt for pre-measured loads when hunting. One of the handiest, most versatile items in this category is the Supreme Quick Loader, which comes in a package of three and is available from Butler Creek Corporation. Although originally designed for muzzleloading rifles, these two-compartment, waterproof plastic containers are ideal for the shotgunner. All you have to do is to reverse the standard procedure and put your loose shot in the "powder" side (it will hold more than two ounces of shot) and pour your pre-measured powder in the "ball" compartment, which will easily carry 3½ drams of FFG, the heaviest load you're likely to use. These handy loaders also have compartments on each end for carrying spare caps.

A second entry in the pre-measured shotgun load category is the Shotgun Tube from Winchester Sutler. These three-part, black, red, and clear plastic tubes are watertight and can carry up to 1¼ ounces of shot and 3 drams of powder. They come twenty in a package and should last for many years. Another handy and inexpensive method for carrying powder and shot are the 35mm plastic film cans from Kodak. If you don't use 35mm film, your local photography store will probably give you all the empty containers you can carry.

Shooting too soon can be just as bad as not shooting at all, especially with one of the big 10-gauge doubles. I take my time in mounting gun as pheasant rises. Had I shot at the moment this photo was taken, there would be little left but feathers — fine for a hat, but not for the table!

They are waterproof and convenient to use. Just be sure you mark each can for either powder or shot, so you know what you are grabbing come reloading time.

Black powder shotgunners desiring to "pour their own" with a little more flair can carry either powder or shot in the new leather-and-wood Shot/Powder flask, manufactured by Uncle Mike's. It too is waterproof.

Speaking of waterproof, one of the problems with early morning and inclement weather hunts, most noticeably during duck season, is the task of keeping moisture off your gun and out of the nipples. After all, it's a known fact that wet powder won't burn, but a wet hunter will, especially if his front-loader misfires. Using a combination of three methods, I have been able to totally eliminate this dilemma. First, obtain a package of Nipple Covers from Butler Creek. These much-needed plastic caps fit over a No. 11 nipple (the size found on most percussion shotguns) and not only seal it from water, but also protect it from being damaged by an accidental drop of the hammer. The Butler Creek Nipple Covers also contain a handy storage space for an extra cap. Next, coat the outside of your gun with a light covering of SS2, a rather amazing water-repellent, protective oil that will last throughout your hunt, doesn't attract dust and will not harm or dry out wood (as many silicone products will). This unique item is available as part of a three-can Muzzle-loaders Care Kit, containing a stock polish, and an in-the-field black powder cleaner (which is also excellent). If you can't find it in your local sporting goods store, you can order it direct from Totally Dependable Products, whose address is listed in Chapter Ten. The third and final product needed to give your shotgun all weather protection is Uncle Mike's Stalking Gun Case. At first, this may sound like a muzzleloading detective story or an Indian Chief's name, but in actuality it is a three-quarter length leather gun case that will cover most single- and double-barrel muzzleloading shotguns up to the trigger and locks, leaving only the stock exposed for quick unsheathing. If your shotgun will be exposed to snow or rain for any length of time, the Stalking Gun Case can help insure the success of your hunt, as well as the longevity of your front-loader.

Practically all muzzleloading shotguns on today's market come with a hooked breech (with Mowrey's being the most notable exception), which simply means that by removing a wedge and taking out the ramrod, the barrel lifts up out of the stock. This makes the gun extremely easy to clean. I have often been chided good-naturedly by fellow writers and hunters because of my fanaticism for immediately cleaning a black powder gun every evening after a hunt, or at least wiping it down if I haven't shot it. However, in more than twenty-five years of black powder shooting, I have never had a gun misfire because of dirt or corrosion. Shotgunning is rarely an overnight venture, but even so, I always carry a cleaning kit in the car, just in case. Two of the most compact and complete black powder shotgun cleaning kits available on today's market are an English Shotgun Cleaning Kit which comes packed in a compact see-through plastic tube and is sold by Dixie Gun Works, and Hoppe's Black Powder Gun Cleaning Kit, which is contained in a convenient black plastic box and is available from most gun stores. Both kits contain an ample supply of solvent, oil, brushes, and patches. The Dixie English kit features a three-piece wooden cleaning rod, while the Hoppe's kit has a four-piece aluminum rod. From personal experience, I can recommend either kit, depending on your preference for metal or wood cleaning rods.

The hunting techniques of muzzleloading scattergunning are basically the same as with those "other" shotguns using ready-made ammunition: keep your head down low to the stock and against it, shoot with both eyes open, and remember, you are *pointing* with the front bead, not aiming it. By the very nature of his sport, the blackpowder shotgunner is a bit more relaxed; his legs are slightly bent, his body loose, and he should lean into the shot to help absorb recoil. For the muzzleloader, it takes a few fractions of a second longer for the hammer to fall, strike the cap, detonate the powder, and have the shot leave the barrel. That means a little more care should be taken in leading fast-flying birds, such as doves, which travel 70 feet per second, or geese, which can hit 90 fps. Personally, I shoot with what I call a "maintained lead," by keeping the muzzle of my shotgun continuously in front of the bird, rather than swinging past him and then firing. I also like to snap shoot at small game and find that I am usually better at bagging fur than feathers. It all depends on what you like and how you shoot. In all cases, black-

Properly outfitted for upland hunting. All elements are carried in bush coat, leaving arms and body free to swing up for shot at squirrel.

powder shotgunning is not like many other shooting sports: there is no competition, no pressure. It is simply meant to be enjoyed.

Obviously, hunting with a muzzleloading shotgun has come a long way since the 1750's. In fact, it is somewhat ironic that today, the sport is beginning to attract a greater number of shooters than at any other time in its 200-plus year history. And no wonder; there are more black powder shotgunners today than ever before, and in many cases, the hunting has never been better. Through the efforts of national organizations such as Ducks Unlimited and local sportsmen's associations, many game species have actually increased in number, making shotgunning all the more productive. In addition, unlike his big game brethren, the muzzleloading scattergunner doesn't have to spend a week away from home or hire a guide in order to enjoy his sport. His charcoal-burning fun can be as close as the "back forty," or an open field just a few hours drive away. Additionally, his gun and equipment, while evoking the memories of the

Waterfowlers can relive the past by shooting over these authentic re-creations of nineteenth century decoys made by Tom Taber's Old River Place. Unlike many decorator ducks on the market, these handmade replicas are working "deke's" and after a few seasons they'll probably be hard to tell from the originals.

past, have never been safer, or more up-to-date. Perhaps then, *these* are the golden years of black powder shotgunning! The celebrated era of 150 years ago merely set the stage for today, and now the muzzleloading shotgunner can realize the full pleasure of this historic sport. Indeed, we are fortunate to be living in both a time and a country that permits us to enjoy muzzleloading shotgunning to its fullest.

PACK A PISTOL

O ften regarded as simply a "fun gun," and relegated to the informal ranks of casual plinking, the flintlock and caplock pistol offers a viable alternative for the hunter seeking additional challenge and satisfaction from his sport. Of equal importance is the black powder pistol's role in providing an extra emergency backup for the hunter whose long gun, for one reason or another, fails to perform its task; it is also a mercifully fast method of providing the *coup de grace* for a game animal that is down but not yet out. However, be sure to check the hunting laws before carrying a black powder pistol during big game season; in some states, this time-honored practice is illegal.

Sometimes ignored by modern mountain men, the black powder pistol was widely used throughout American history. Meriwether Lewis and William Clark each carried a pair of flintlock belt guns on their famed expedition into former French territory along the Mississippi; in the 1840's, Kit Carson used to sleep with two half-cocked Colt revolvers under his bedroll. Still later, Bill Hickok's swift and deadly use of his twin .36 Navy Colts created a legend that survived his sudden death.

Today, the muzzleloading hunter may capture the added adventure the black powder pistol affords by choosing from two basic styles: the flintlock or percussion single shot, or the percussion revolver. Like most things in life, there are good and bad points for

either selection. The single shot pistols can generally digest a heftier charge of black powder and normally sport larger bores, thereby giving them greater striking energy (i.e., killing power) for their one shot. However, that one shot is all you get until you reload, just as with a muzzleloading rifle. The caplock revolver, on the other hand, is capable of firing six shots without reloading. Unfortunately, the system literally has its hangups, as bits of spent cap are often prone to drop down between hammer or cylinder and frame, thereby jamming the gun for the next round. Of even more importance to the hunter is the little-realized fact that although the Colts and Remingtons have gone down in history as man-killers, in reality they have extremely limited killing power. The chambers of even the largest wheelgun, the mighty and monstrously heavy Colt Walker, can hold only 60 grains of powder (equivalent to the charges I sometimes

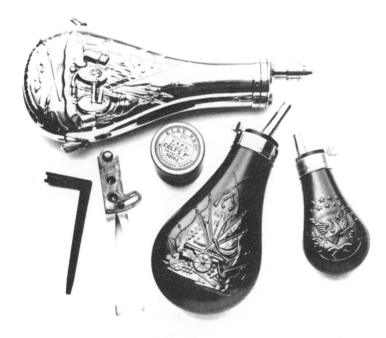

A few traditional accessories: powder flasks for horse, holster, and pocket pistols, combination nipple wrench and screwdriver (often subject to breakage and best left at home) two-cavity bullet mold (watch out, those brass handles get *hot!*) and percussion caps.

use in my TVA squirrel rifle), hardly a potent hunting charge for anything larger than coyotes at close range.

Although the black powder handgun has proven to be an effective game-getter for furbearers such as rabbits, woodchucks, squirrels, and even wolves, *under no circumstances should it ever be considered a big game weapon.* The stopping power just is not there. For example, the Colt .44 Dragoon, by far the largest black powder revolver a hunter can conveniently pack without sinking into the ground, fires its 135-grain round ball, backed by 40 grains of FFFG, with a muzzle velocity of only 196 foot pounds of energy, or about 40 foot pounds *less* than a .38 Special. That puts it into the small game category, in spite of its thunderous roar and over 4 pounds of weight. Further evidence of the black powder handgun's limitations in the hunting field was brought to my attention a while back, when a well-known and experienced muzzleloading hunter tried to take a wild boar with a replica Walker. As the tale was later told to me by the individual, using full charges the hunter hit the boar broadside with a well-aimed shot just 40 feet away. Thereupon commenced a frantic 10-mile chase and even then, that snarling, snapping boar required three more shots from the Walker to finish him. Of course, there are exceptions to every rule, and I am sure someone, somewhere, at sometime has probably dropped a trophy bull elephant with a single shot from his .31 Wells Fargo pocket pistol. But I would not want to try it, nor should any hunter who values not only his life, but his responsibility to take game swiftly and cleanly.

Used within its limitations, however, the black powder pistol can be an effective means for bagging extra meat, such as rabbits or grouse, for the camp. When loaded with shot, instead of round ball, the revolver or single shot can also make an ideal trail gun for dispatching snakes and other unwanted vermin at close range, up to 10 feet. As a teenager in Arizona, I bagged many a jackrabbit with an original .36 Navy Colt that I had purchased for less money than it takes to buy a fifth of Jack Daniels today. I still enjoy packing a cap and ball out to the high desert during hunting season to see what might pop up between me and the muzzle of my 1860 Army or Colt reissue .36 Navy. On big game hunts, I always have one of the larger-bored pistols, usually a Western Arms Tucker & Sherrard .44 Dragoon, in a holster when on horseback, or a Colt Army when on foot. And for off-season varminting, nothing beats sitting in a comfortable position on a hill and potting 'chucks or crows with one of the single shot pistols, be it flintlock (a challenge in itself) or percussion.

Unlike the muzzleloading rifle hunter, the type of game-getting you plan to do will probably not dictate the pistol you choose, as all are relatively limited to the same size of game they can adequately take. Therefore, personal taste and physical appearance will play an even more obvious role in your selection of a pistol (in a rifle, this tends to be more subliminal). Because the cap and ball revolver is by far the most widely used black powder handgun today, let's discuss it first.

Aside from the Old West romance traditionally associated with these guns, their overwhelming selection by shooters is due to their greater capacity for firepower, which, not surprisingly, is the very same factor that made them so popular over a century ago. But it should be pointed out that a black powder revolver will start to

Pistol's close-range usage as a camp or trail gun becomes more versatile when loaded with shot instead of ball.

gum up after twelve to eighteen shots (depending on the gun and the size of the charge you are using), so if you plan to spend some time in heavily-infested small game country, take along a wooden dowel and a small brass hammer to tap out the wedge for the open frame Colt-style guns, and some solvent and a rag to wipe off the fouling. The solid-frame, Remington-style revolvers do not require a wedge to be driven out for cleaning, and they break down much easier. It has been my experience that they also will foul up faster, making the hammer difficult to cock and hindering cylinder rotation until they are finally field stripped and wiped clean with a solvent-soaked rag. A small cleaning rod and combination pistol nipple wrench-and-pick, such as sold by Uncle Mike's, is not a bad item to take along for either style of revolver.

The serious hunter should not even consider a brass-framed revolver. Although they look pretty, and harken back to the days when the Confederacy had to melt down churchbells to make armament, these guns will generally shoot loose after a few hundred rounds, an unavoidable situation caused by the softness of the brass. It is also a shiny metal, and has no place in the hunter's camp, as discussed in Chapter Two. For your sidearm, select one of the quality all-steel replicas.

In addition to quality, safety is of key concern for the hunter. When carrying a holstered cap and ball revolver in the field, it is standard practice to emulate the experienced pistoleers who came before us: always rest the hammer on an uncapped nipple over an empty or previously fired chamber. Otherwise, a sharp blow to the hammer (should your pistol accidentally fall out of your holster or bang against a tree) could fire the gun, and you *know* where that muzzle might be pointed! Another safety precaution that was advertised by the gun manufacturers to the frontiersmen was to rest the hammer on one of the shallow "pins" (for Colt revolvers) or in the grooves (for Remington) located in the cyclinder between each nipple. However, I have found that this practice can occasionally throw your revolver out of time when cocking the piece rapidly, causing the chamber and nipple to "skip" past their proper alignment with the hammer and barrel. The result, of course, is a misfire. Keeping the hammer down on an uncapped, uncharged chamber is still the safest way of carrying a six-gun, which means that it really becomes a five-shot revolver, which still should be adequate for most small-game hunting situations. In the nineteenth century, the only time a frontiersman kept all six chambers loaded was when he was expecting "big trouble," and if that is ever the case with today's muzzleloading hunter, then he had better be carrying a hard-shooting, large caliber rifle as well as his pistol.

There are many different types of percussion revolvers on the market today, but the most practical choices for the hunter are the Colt and Remington copies. Other replicas have certain design flaws that make them as unsuitable today as they were in the 1860's: awkward grips, hammer spur too long to cock conveniently, protruding pins in the loading lever, and so on. The guns may be well made, but the muzzleloading hunter's criteria demands more than that; his guns must also be functional.

Although it seems there are almost as many cap and ball manufacturers today as there were 150 years ago, the best quality guns come from a handful of firms such as Allen Arms, Lyman, Navy Arms Co., and Euroarms. Colt is also producing excellent reissues of their original designs, but they are slightly higher in price than the other manufacturers. Certain variations of standard guns, such as the stainless steel models and Dixie Gun Works' folding leaf sight Dragoon, are also worthy of consideration by the hunter, and we will be reviewing these guns in this chapter also.

In discussing each revolver for hunting, primary attention should be given to caliber. Therefore, any serious hunter must totally discount the diminutive .31 caliber pocket pistols, no matter how well made they are or how convenient they may be to carry. With their 12-grain powder charge and 30 foot pounds of striking energy, they should only be used during the mosquito season in Texas, and even then, more than one shot may be required.

In terms of caliber then, the next size up is the .36, which is available in either the open-frame Colt Navy style, or the solid-frame Remington, which features a top strap. Personally, I find the Navy easier to cock and shoot. Its superb plow-handle grip, one of the most refined designs to come out of the black powder era, makes aiming with this revolver almost as natural as pointing with your finger. The Navy, like all Colt-style cap and balls, has a rear sight "V" milled into the hammer, with a brass bead serving as the front sight. Simply translated, that means these sights are not meant to be used at all, for the point of aim can change with hammer wear and can even be affected by the amount of force used to drive in the barrel wedge. No, the Navy, like all open-top designs, is strictly a pointing gun, a technique we will discuss a little later on in this chapter. The Remington has a slightly more reliable sighting system, consisting of a rear sight channel milled along the top strap; the front sight is a small tab of steel. Even this fixed sight is not conducive to accurate shooting, but it has the advantage of not shifting due to wear every time the gun is taken apart for cleaning.

In addition to the full-framed versions of the .36s, Allen Arms, Navy and Colt also make the smaller "pocket pistol" models, most notably the 1862 Pocket Navy and Pocket Police, which look like scaled-down models of the 1851 Navy and 1860 Army, respectively. Due to their reduced sizes, the cylinders of these guns hold only five shots. This should not be of concern to the small game hunter, for I have rarely had an occasion to empty my cap and ball revolver at

Hunters with small hands often prefer small-framed revolvers, such as this Allen Arms 1862 Pocket Police in .36 caliber. Similar revolvers are made by Navy Arms and Colt.

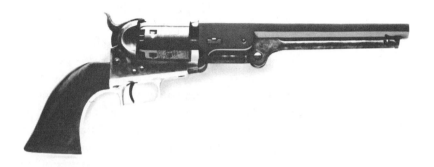

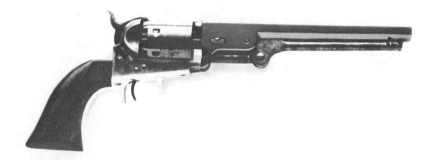

(Top) Colt 1851 Navy is one of the best "pointing" revolvers. *(Bottom)* 1861 Navy is a .36 caliber revolver that is slightly smaller than the '51, but it shoots the same load.

anything; if I did not hit what I was aiming at with the first two shots, it was long gone before I ever got the third shot off.

The pocket models can easily hold from 15 to 20 grains of FFFG or Pyrodex P, making them almost as potent as the larger-framed 1851 Navy. Moreover, they are easier to carry, as they come in 4½-, 5½-, and 6½-inch barrel lengths. I have a little 4½-inch Pocket Police that I take with me when out small game hunting with a rifle, just to give me that "extra edge" should I need it. Carried on a belt in a cross-draw holster, you hardly know it is there. The pocket models also make ideal guns for shooters with small hands, which takes in women and children. As one manufacturer's wife so descriptively stated, the pocket models are probably the "cutest" of all the C & B revolvers.

The .36 is an extremely accurate caliber; firing from a rest at 25 yards, it is possible to place all five shots within a 1½-inch circle. Powered by an average load in the 1851 Navy of 22 grains of powder, the 70-grain round ball leaves the muzzle at 710 feet per second and has a striking energy of 78 foot pounds. A practiced hunter can perform wonders on jackrabbits, squirrels and similar sized creatures out to about 50 yards; beyond that, the round ball begins to stray, and placing your hits in a vital zone becomes more a matter of luck.

The massive 4½-pound Colt Walker is much too heavy and cumbersome for practical hunting, although it certainly is capable of taking game. Here, Dixie's reproduction almost dwarfs Southern Illinois woodchuck that was felled by 45 grains of FFFG, two wads, and a .454 round ball, at a range of 25 yards. Looks like the gun is weighing the poor fellow down. Photo courtesy of Toby Bridges.

Improved rachet design of 1860 Army's loading lever makes it as popular today as it was during the War Between the States. Note shooter's trigger finger *outside* the guard while she is loading, a common safety practice among experienced hunters.

Although I used to do small game handgunning with a .36 Colt Navy reissue, I have since adopted the .44 as my favorite hunting sidearm, primarily due to the greater striking force of the 128-grain ball. The .44s come in two basic sizes: the 1860 Colt and 1858 Remington belt (or holster) models, and the larger, heavier horse pistols, the Dragoons. As I have said, there is a larger size yet, the 4½-pound Colt Walker, but the excessive weight of this gun, plus the fact that it lacks many of the refinements of the later models (i.e., rectangular locking lugs on the cyclinder and a catch on the barrel to keep the loading lever from dropping down during recoil, thereby jamming cylinder rotation for what could be a very important sec-

The many varieties of the famous 1860 Army *(top to bottom)* Euroarms Stainless Steel, Dixie's fluted model, and Euroarms 5½-inch barrel model. In addition, the "standard" blued and case-hardened version with 7½-inch barrel is available from Allen Arms, Navy Arms and Euroarms.

ond shot) make this gun unsuitable for practical black powder hunting, although it is definitely capable of taking game.

Of the belt model .44s, the 1860 Army is by far my favorite, even though the effectiveness of the elongated grips, originally designed to help absorb recoil, is open to question. I would much prefer this same gun if it were fitted with Navy grips. Not as easy-pointing as the Navy, it is somehow more attractive and epitomizes the highest state-of-the-art in black powder design. Its unique creeping ratchet loading lever does not jam up, as the other Colt-style guns are occasionally prone to do, and the smooth flowing lines of the 7½-inch barrel make it look as if it came out of the art-deco 1920's rather than the era of the Great Rebellion.

Two variations of the 1860 Army, both produced by Euroarms, are worthy of additional consideration for the hunter. The first version is similar to the standard Army, but the barrel and loading lever have been shortened to 5½ inches, making the gun 3 ounces lighter and much easier to carry. I have fitted one of these guns with Navy

Solid frame Remington is available in either .44 caliber *(shown)* or a slightly scaled-down .36

Target version of the Remington features adjustable sights, something that originals of this gun did not have.

Ruger Old Army .44 is first completely new cap and ball revolver to come along in over one hundred years. It is shown here in the stainless steel version.

grips and have found it ideal for packing on my hunts as a back-up revolver.

The second Euroarms version of the 1860 is their stainless steel version of the standard 7½-inch barrel model. For the hunter residing in humid climates, or for wet weather forays or lengthy stays in the field, the stainless 1860 can justify its slightly higher cost. It should be pointed out that even a black powder stainless gun will eventually fall prey to rust and corrosion, if neglected for any length of time, but it will take longer for the discoloration and pitting to get started.

Another version of the .44 belt pistol is the 1858 Remington, which also comes in both a blued and a stainless steel model. Navy Arms and Allen Arms produce both the .36 and .44 Remington revolvers in a special "target model" variation, featuring adjustable rear sights, which aids tremendously in improving the accuracy of these guns especially if the hunter gets into a good, solid sitting position and utilizes a steady, two-handed hold. However, some hunters, preferring the open-topped Colt designs, have dovetailed adjustable open sights into the rear of the barrel flats, which at least keeps the rear sight in constant alignment with the front sight, something the hammer-notch system fails to do.

There is a third style of .44 in the "belt pistol" size, although this particular revolver is not a replica of any previously-existing firearm. Nonetheless, it is so well designed that it should be seriously considered for the muzzleloading handgun hunter. This modern cap and ball revolver (the first really new black powder revolver to be developed since the advent of the cartridge gun) is manufactured by Sturm, Ruger & Company and is simply called the Old Army. It has solid-frame construction with an adjustable rear sight and a modern ramp front sight. The loading lever is an all-new, jam-free design, and the gun sports plow-handle grips reminiscent of the Colt Navy. However, that, plus the fact that it shoots black powder, are the only items that the Old Army has in common with the old-timers. The rest of the gun is all modern. It features a coiled mainspring (rather than the more traditional flat spring) and comes in either blued or stainless steel variations. It is an excellent black

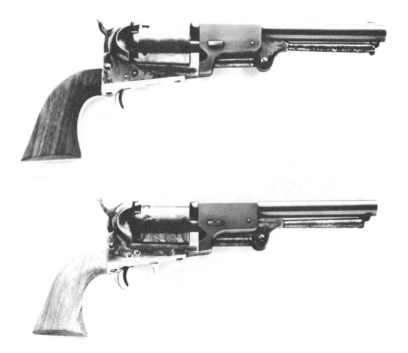

Second and Third Model Colt Dragoons are more advanced in design than the First Model, and should be the only practical choices for the hunter who favors this big horse pistol.

powder revolver whose only fault is the fact that there is no sense of history or nostalgia connected to its design. But then, I imagine that is what folks said about the Colt 1860 Army when it first came out.

No matter which of these three .44s you select, you will have a potent friend at your side. The chambers of either the 1860 Army or the 1858 Remington revolvers easily take a 28-grain hunting load of powder (the Ruger can handle slightly more) which propels the .44 caliber round ball at 736 feet per second and hits with a force of 154 foot pounds, almost double that of the .36s. The greater bullet energy is due to the larger ball size (the actual powder charge is only 6 grains higher).

The larger-framed .44 revolvers are commonly called horse pistols, and with good reason; they were originally intended to be carried in twin saddle holsters by mounted U.S. Dragoons. Hence their name. These big guns are my favorite as far as looks and romance are concerned, even though they are far from being practical. But then, I did say that personal taste was the dominant factor in

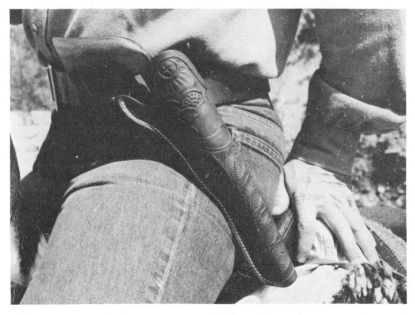

Most practical way for horsemen to wear gun is the crossdraw.

selecting a hunting handgun. I just happen to like the way they look and feel, especially the square-backed Second Model. There is also a Dragoon Third Model, which features a rounded trigger guard. Hunters should ignore the early first model; it has the less-efficient, oval-looking slots on the cylinder, a less-secure locking latch holding the loading lever under the barrel, and a weaker "V"-shaped mainspring. It was because of these design difficulties that the Second and Third models were invented, so why hamper your gun's performance? Buy the improved models!

In keeping with the Dragoon's original purpose, I habitually carry a Second Model variation with me as a sidearm when big game hunting on horseback. I do this not so much out of allegiance to tradition, as for practicality; straddling a saddle is the only way I can carry this 4¼-pound behemoth all day without having it drag my pants down over my boots. Besides, I like its firepower, by far one of the most potent of all the black powder revolvers. Loaded with 40 grains of FFFG, the 135-grain lead ball has a muzzle velocity of 830 feet per second and strikes with 207 foot pounds of energy, not hardly enough to qualify for javelina or deer, but plenty powerful for a surefire finishing shot or for plinking coyotes within a 50–75 yard range limitation, if you place your shots in vital areas.

The Second Model Dragoons are made only by Colt and Allen Arms. The model I carry is an Allen Arms Confederate variation called the Tucker & Sherrard, a beautifully-made gun that is just different enough (i.e., Texas Star cylinder etching) to set it apart from the more commonly seen Colt design. And I do like individuality in my guns—helps 'em shoot better! Third model Dragoons are produced by Colt, Allen Arms, and Dixie Gun Works, whose model has a useful set of flip-up leaf sights affixed to the barrel, making them somewhat more accurate than the hammer-notch sight.

Like the originals from which they were copied, all replica cap and ball revolvers tend to shoot high, usually 2 or 3 inches from point-of-aim at 25 yards. If you still insist on using those Colt-type hammer-notch sights after all that I have told you, your best bet is to have a gunsmith build up the brass front sight, which will lower your point-of-aim.

As a supposed "aid" to accuracy, the frames of some cap and ball revolvers, most notably the 1851 Navy, 1860 Army and a few of the Dragoons, come designed or "cut" for use with a detachable shoulder stock. The shoulder-stocked revolver is not for the muzzle-loading hunter, or anyone else who wants to keep his cheek on his face. The flash and escaping gases from the sides of the cylinder are easy to ignore when fired at arm's length. When the revolver is affixed to a shoulder stock, however, and the breech end is tucked up next to your face, every pull of the trigger results in a slap from Madam Gunpowder that is sure to cause flinching, and fragments of flying caps can make the shooter look like he just came out of the Battle of Bull Run. Attach those stocks only to wall-hangers, never on a hunting revolver.

Fixed or adjustable stocks and sights aside, the best way to hunt with the black powder revolver is point shooting, an old-time method once used by trick shooters in Buffalo Bill's Wild West Show. It must be remembered that the handgun is still a close-range hunting weapon at best. In point shooting, the gun is not fired from the hip (although it may appear that way) but rather, is brought up so that as the eye is looking at the fur-bearing "target," the tip of the barrel also comes into view, and the hunter is also looking *over* the barrel and sights, not at them. Thus, an imaginary triangle is formed between your line of sight to the target and a straight line leading from your gun barrel to the target. Everything converges on the target, including the bullet, if you have point-shot correctly, and this includes knowing just when to pull the trigger and ascertaining how much lead to give the target if it is moving. In this respect, point shooting is a little like shotgunning. Of course, the "sights," such as they are, can always be used, but I find point shooting more fun. It does take a lot of practice, but that is part of the enjoyment of constantly perfecting your hunting skills. It's also a good excuse to go out and burn some powder during the off-season.

Because of varying manufacturing tolerances, a cap and ball revolver may come from the factory with an action that is rougher than you would like. This may not be of too much concern for the plinker, but for a hunting gun it should not be condoned.

Most actions will smooth up slightly with use, but it usually takes about fifty to a hundred shots to get the gun properly "broken in." I find a few drops of Teflon-coated TufOil inside the action will help the breaking-in process along somewhat. Extremely rough ac-

Point shooting takes practice, but it is one of the most practical ways to hunt with fixed-sight revolvers.

Multiple discharges can be prevented by using one of three methods: From left to right, Ox-Yoke Original Wonder Wads, felt-treated wads from Dixie, or Butler Creek plastic pistol patches. Also shown is Dixie Gun Works' 3rd Model Dragoon with folding leaf sights.

tions, however, may require a tune-up visit at the local gunsmith. If nothing else, you may just want to smooth off some of the rough edges of the bolt, hand, and trigger spur with a Swiss file. And be sure to clean out all of that Vaseline-type grease that is squeezed into every crevice of your revolver by some manufacturers. The stuff can actually gum up your action if it mixes with enough dirt and it *will* freeze in cold weather. RIG makes a fine aerosol de-greaser that will blast most of the greasy gunk out of the smallest nooks and crannies of your gun, but be sure to coat the metal with a light gun oil afterwards to prevent rust.

Speaking of grease, it should be remembered that all black powder revolvers are subject to multiple discharges, a rather spectacular and potentially dangerous event caused by the flash from one cylinder jumping over into the next chamber and setting off the other charges in your gun. This thunderous experience has traditionally been avoided by covering the loaded chambers with grease, a method which is totally impractical for the hunter, who carries his holstered cap and ball in the field all day. In the summer, the grease will melt and soak his holster, if not his powder charges. In the winter, cold-numbed fingers make the application of grease an awkward and time-consuming venture. And no matter what the season, it is always messy. Far better methods — three of them — are illustrated in this chapter, and they all involve the principle of separating the powder and ball with a non-combustible felt or plastic wad. It takes a little more time in loading, but it definitely will make the sport of handgun hunting a safer one and you will be able to concentrate on placing your shots one at a time, rather than all at once.

Of course, no worries of multiple discharges plague the single-shot pistoleer. And the fact that there is no gas escaping between cylinder and barrel means revolver-type loads of powder and ball will have more velocity and striking energy when fired from a single shot. However, chances are you will be firing heavier loads, for the thick-walled construction of the barrel and breech areas of most single shots usually mean that more powder can be loaded and safely fired than a revolver would ever permit. Still, excess charges should be avoided for safety's sake and in all cases, manufacturer's recommended loads should be followed. More power and less susceptibility to misfires (compared with revolvers) make the ol' one-shot something to be seriously considered by today's muzzleloading hunter.

The single shot pistols were on the shooting scene long before revolvers and were usually carried as a last-ditch personal defense weapon by gentlemen of means. They were never thought of as a

Toby Bridges outfitted this Thompson/Center .45 Patriot with a scope and found it to be an ideal small game-getting rig.

legitimate hunting weapon. Fortunately for the black powder hunter of today, all that has changed, although it only has been recently that we have had an adequate variety of re-created horse pistols from which to choose. Of course, the Thompson/Center Patriot has been around for years. With its hooded front and adjustable rear sights, double-set triggers and comfortable balance, this .45 caliber percussion, "augmented dueler" is wonderfully accurate for informal game-taking. Unfortunately, the same sights that make it such an accurate shooter also hamper its use for the hunter transporting it afield, for the hooded front sight and sharply protruding rear aperture make the Patriot difficult to withdraw from one's belt without getting it snagged and appearing as if you are trying to yank yourself off of your own feet! In all fairness, it should be pointed out that the Patriot was not designed as a belt gun; a modern compilation of the nineteenth century dueler and gallery (target) pistol, it is inherently accurate. Loaded with a .440 patched round ball and backed by 35 grains of FFFG or Pyrodex P, it develops a muzzle velocity of 900 feet per second, greater than the mightiest Dragoon revolver. Switching from the lightweight 127-grain round ball to the heavier 220-grain unpatched greased Maxi-Ball results in approximately 10 per cent less muzzle velocity but substantially greater killing power. Consequently, the Patriot makes a formidable handgun for the hunter who does not have to pack it very far and likes to still hunt. Because of its updated design, the Patriot is the modern-day single shot counterpart of Ruger's Old Army. If your handgunning tastes run to the more traditional, then you will more probably find favor with the rest of the single shots currently available, as they are almost all mirror-like, well-made copies of guns that existed in our muzzleloading past.

The three earliest versions available to the muzzleloading hunter, logically enough, are flintlocks, and they represent an additional challenge by the very nature of their ignition systems. Flintlock rifles are normally carried more or less parallel to the ground, thereby hindering accidental loss or movement of the priming charge away from the touch-hole. The hand-held flinter, however, is much more mobile; when carried in a belt the priming charge shifts forward, when raised to take aim or to cock, the charge moves to the rear. In brief, those tiny grains of FFFFG shift around in the flashpan about as much as an egg in a well-greased frying pan. All this means is that the flintlock handgunner had better take extra care to check his priming charge before pulling the trigger or he will merely be making sparks.

Navy Arms has the distinction of producing the first authentic copy of a 1770's era flintlock pistol for the mass market, even though the gun is only available in limited numbers. It is a recreation of the British Flint Dragoon Pistol, a .614 smoothbore. True to the originals, the gun has no sights and is "aimed" (I use that term loosely) by sighting down the foot-long barrel. Firing a patched round ball, this hand-held flinter can hit a pumpkin-sized target out to 25 yards. However, the British Dragoon is far more effective when stoked up with No.6 or No.4 shot, as the bore is only slightly larger than 20 gauge. That makes it ideal for close range varminting and can put a lot of smoke-filled action into your next rabbit hunt. (You will have to cut your own over-powder and over-shot wads from cardboard, however.) I've never been able to get close enough to feathered game to take a poke at them with this long barreled flintlock, but that is not to say it cannot be done. You should certainly try it if you are fortunate enough to stick one of these Revolutionary sidearms in your weapons belt.

In terms of design, the British Dragoon was accurate enough to be selected as one of the flintlocks used for the restoration of the Governor's Palace at Colonial Williamsburg. However, in terms of

Navy Arms British Flint Dragoon.

shooting accuracy, Navy's Model 1806 Harper's Ferry Flintlock has it beat. This early mountain man single shot features a .58 rifled barrel with fixed sights, making it surprisingly accurate at ranges up to 50 yards. It is a natural back-up gun for the hunter with a .58 flintlock rifle.

For those hunters following in the fur trapper's footsteps, Green River Forge, Ltd. makes a superb flintlock Hudson's Bay Factor's Pistol, the type carried by booshways in the Rocky Mountains during the early 1800's. Probably one of the best made replicas on the market, this gun is not easy to obtain, as it is individually hand-made on a custom basis, meaning you might have a wait of six

The single shot pistol for the hunter is a direct descendant of the big bore Howdah pistols used years ago by big game hunters in Africa needing a last-ditch, close-range insurance policy. For flintlock aficionados, Navy Arms .58 caliber Harper's Ferry fills the bill and the hand.

Green River Forge Factor's Pistol features safety catch, waterproof pan and authentic hand craftsmanship.

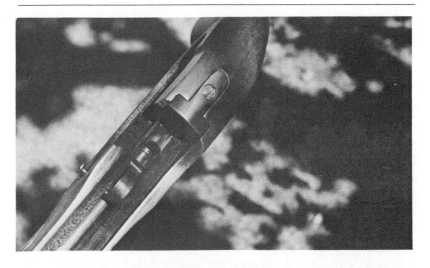

Many single shots, such as CVA's Mountain Pistol feature hooked breech (note also the ramrod retaining spring—an exclusive feature), and clean-out screw.

months to a year to enjoy its quality. The Factor's Pistol is available in either 20 gauge (.595 ball) smoothbore or in .50 caliber with a rifled barrel, which I have as a companion piece to my .50 caliber Dixie Tennessee Mountain Rifle. Like the originals, the Factor's Pistol has all the luxury features a "working gun" of the period should sport: sliding hammer safety catch, waterproof pan, excellent balance, and a belt hook which eliminates the need for a holster (and is much more convenient than simply shoving the gun in your belt). The hooked breech makes this flinter easy to clean, but the token front sight and lack of a rear sight places the same range limitations on the Factor's Pistol as there are on the larger British Dragoon.

Moving into the percussion era of the fur trader's pistols, the hunter can choose from what I consider to be two of the most practical single shot muzzleloading handguns on today's market: the Lyman Plains Pistol (which is available in either .50 or .54 caliber, to go along as a companion piece with their Great Plains Rifle, a commendable feature) and the CVA Mountain Pistol, which only comes in .50 caliber. Both guns are well made, reliable and accurate and your final decision will probably be dictated by a combination of price, availability, and a personal preference for some of the design differences. For example, the CVA product features a flat mainspring and browned barrel, while Lyman uses a coiled spring and blued metalwork. Both Hawken-styled pistols have a hooked breech for easy barrel removal for cleaning, fixed front and rear sights, and belt hooks, although CVA supplies a brown metal plug for the stock if you do not want the hook on your gun. However, the balance of both pistols is different, and before making your final selection, I recommend visiting your local black powder dealer and hefting each gun to find out which one is best for you.

If aiming and accuracy are your forte and you take great pride in being able to consistently make clean-kill head shots on even the smallest of critters, then I highly recommend the Navy Arms Le

Lyman's Plains Pistol features coil mainspring and spring-tension trigger to prevent rattling.

Navy Arms Le Page provides varmint-getting accuracy, but remember to pack along a ramrod.

Page Dueling Pistol. An 1860's style percussion argument solver, the Le Page is not a hunting handgun in the pure sense of the word, but it is accurate. It has a 9-inch rifled barrel in .44 caliber, crowned with adjustable front and rear sights. The single-set adjustable trigger and well contoured, hand-checkered grip puts this pistol in the same class as the Patriot as far as shot placement is concerned, although it does not come with a ramrod. It is designed as more of a "city" gun and therefore, lacks some of the "wilderness romance" of its other single shot brethren.

Finally, saving the biggest percussion single shot for the last, we come to the .58 Harper's Ferry 1855 Dragoon Pistol made by Navy Arms. This gun is the caplock cousin to the Harper's Ferry Flinter. Its bore size and ignition system make it the ideal back-up gun for either the .58 CVA Big Bore or the .58 Kodiak rifle. The rear sight consists of two fold-over leafs, allegedly for long and short-range shooting, but I suggest you square off the notch of one of the sights so that you know where it's shooting, and leave it there. The steel ramrod of the Harper's Ferry is permanently attached to the barrel via a swivel, which means losing the rod is virtually impossible (unless, of course, you lose the gun!). The 11¾-inch barrel of the Model 1855 makes it noticeably muzzle-heavy, and its grips, overly contoured for the average hand, render it difficult to hold steady for offhand shooting. However, one of the unique features about this heavy-duty horse pistol is that, like the originals, it comes with a detachable shoulder stock, which aids shot placement immensely. Unlike the poorly contrived detachable shoulder stocks on the Civil War era revolvers, the Harper's Ferry stock works. The reason is that the breech of the single shot pistol is constructed like that of a rifle; there is no opening near the shooter's face (other than the nipple) to permit escaping flame and gas to slap him around. Thus, the

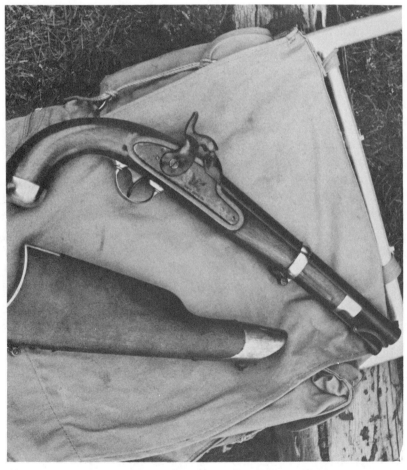

This Model 1855 Harper's Ferry .58 Pistol with detachable shoulder stock is just the combination for the backpacking hunter. Rifled pistol assembles into an 11¾-inch barrel carbine in less than 30 seconds.

somewhat awkward Model 1855 quickly and easily can be transformed into a mini-carbine, making it ideal for backpackers and other hunters who want the steadiness of a rifle without the bulk, and the convenience of a pistol with a little more aiming potential.

All of the above-listed pistols (with the exception of the Patriot) are intended to be used with round ball only. Do not attempt to fire a Mini- or Maxi-Ball in these revolvers as excessive pressures may result. Even though the conical slugs are better game-getters, the size of quarry limited to the uae of the pistol does not warrant this extra killing power. I have found the best hunting loads in most single shot pistols to range between 35 and 60 grains of FFFG (although FFG can be used in the .58 Harper's Ferry), or Pyrodex P. Start with light loads and work your way up gradually to achieve optimum balance between accuracy and firepower. In no case should you exceed the manufacturer's recommendations, however. In the single shots, always use a patched ball for maximum accuracy (see Hunter's Helpers - Chapter Six, for hints on how to make sure your flintlock or percussion will speak when you tell it to). It is fairly certain that, due to the large diameters of the lead balls you will be throwing, any rabbit- to coyote-sized game that gets hit in a vital area will end up in your cooking pot or taxidermy shop.

Knowing where to properly place your bullet becomes more critical when using your pistol for administering the final shot to a game animal that has already been dropped. That animal must not suffer if the hunter is to retain his noble title. Therefore, the shot must be accurate, deadly, and at close range. If you are hunting strictly for meat, then a head shot, directly into the brain, is the only one to take. However, if you are after a trophy as well as meat, then the bullet must pass through the spine, preferably at the base of the neck. Always fire from *behind* the animal, never in front, where you might be in direct danger from hooves, antlers, or horns.

When using the single shot pistol primarily as a back-up weapon for your rifle, it is a good idea to try and carry identical calibers for both guns. That way there is less chance of mixing up balls of different sizes when rushing for that fast second shot. Of course, hunters carrying cap and ball revolvers do not have this problem, as extra charges are rarely needed or used when the gun is relegated strictly to backup work. When hunting small game with the .36

Mowrey or TVA squirrel guns, the .36 Colt and Remington balls will not work, for they must measure slightly more than bore size in order to assure a good gas seal (in fact, when you press the ball into the revolver's chamber with the loading lever, you should see a thin ring of lead being shaved off around the perimeter. Conversely, seating a single shot's patched ball is the same as loading a round ball rifle). As a reference guide for the hunter, here is a chart of the proper ball sizes for the guns listed in this chapter. Remember, revolvers do not require patches; single shots do.

Type of Gun	Calibre of Ball (use soft lead only)
.36 Revolver	.376
.44 Revolver	.441
(medium frame)	
1860 Army	
1858 Remington	
.44 Revolver	.457
Ruger Old Army	
.44 Revolver (large frame)	.445
Dragoon	
.45 Patriot	.445 patched ball
.50 Single shot	.490 patched ball
.54 Single shot	.535 patched ball
.58 Single shot	.570 patched ball

As with round ball rifles, always load with the sprue facing up; otherwise, the soft lead will be deformed in loading and accuracy will suffer.

All of the revolvers and single shots, with the exception of the 1855 Harper's Ferry, take the standard No. II cap, the same as most rifles. The Model 1855 requires a musket cap. Therefore, if using this gun as a back-up for your rifle, be sure to take along a musket-sized nipple wrench for emergencies (your rifle's wrench won't fit) and carry the pistol's caps in a separate container.

For the hunter with a revolver, transporting his cap and ball in the field presents no problem except to decide what style of belt and holster he wishes to strap on. Red River Frontier Outfitters make a 100 percent authentic "Slim Jim" style of civilian holster for any of the nineteenth century revolvers (no holsters are made for the Ruger

Red River makes classic "Slim Jim" holsters for cap and ball revolvers *(left and right)* while Bianchi produces an updated "Model 1851 Black Powder" version *(center)* for both Remington and Colt guns.

Old Army). Each holster is hand-styled exactly as originals of the cap and ball era and form-fitted with a copy of the gun for which it is being made. These holsters are custom in the true sense of the word, and may be ordered for right- or left-hand shooters, and either left plain, or decorated with leatherwork that ranges from simple to fancy. They are well worth the money; after carrying your sidearm in a Red River holster for a few hunts, it will be difficult to tell your holster from an original 1860's version. Be sure to allow at least ninety days for completion of your order.

If you do not wish to wait three months to start packing your pistol afield, an excellent ready-made, open-topped black powder holster is produced by Bianchi Gunleather, the Model 1851. This handsome frontier-styled holster fits all medium-frame black powder revolvers, such as the Remington and the '51 and '60 Colts. It is hand-finished, rugged and has an adjustable hammer thong for keeping your revolver on your hip, not on the ground.

Big sturdy pistols demand big sturdy holsters for field wear. My prized No. 12 Tucker and Sherrard Confederate Dragoon by Allen Arms is right at home in this cross-draw holster by The George Lawrence Company. Flap and sewed end provide all-weather protection.

Personally, I prefer open-topped holsters, as they permit easier access to the gun and besides, I like to see a bit of grip poking up out of the leather. However, the hunter who carries his precious cap and ball into rugged country or stormy weather will welcome the protection of the military-styled flap holster. One of the best versions of this model is the 1776 Trophy Holster made by the George Lawrence Company. I have one of these Lawrence holsters, made to fit my dragoons, and can recommend it highly. Not only is the craftsmanship superb, but the flap fastens with a stud; there is no noisy snap to spook game. The holster is available in either plain, basket weave, or flower-carved and comes in brown or black, left- and right-handed styles, and crossdraw, which I find ideal for big horse pistols.

Butt-forward, high-riding, and flapped holsters patterned after those used in the War Between the States are made by Bianchi and

Lawrence, and come complete with belt and cap pouch. You can even choose sides with the Lawrence version by selecting either U.S. or C.S. buckles; John Bianchi has chosen to remain neutral by offering his version with an Indian Wars buckle, but he does have a brown CSA model, too. With either of these well-known firms, you

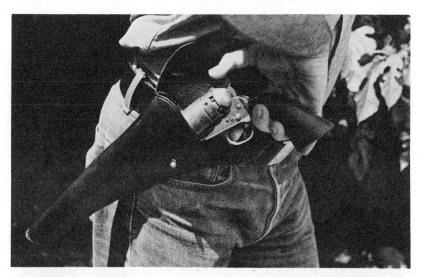

(Top) Civil War styled rigs are fine, but standard "twist draw" is awkward. *(Bottom)* A better system is to order a "military left hand" holster and turn it into a cross draw.

[129]

cannot lose, although as depicted elsewhere in this chapter, I prefer switching the military's "twist draw" to a crossdraw. Just order a left-handed version if you are a right-handed shooter.

Bill Ruger's company makes an updated version of the century-old flap holster. They call it, appropriately enough, the Practical Holster and, unlike some of the others, it *will* fit their Old Army (not surprised, are you?). It will also work for some of the Colt and Remington Revolvers, but not the big Dragoons. No noisy snaps on this holster, either, just a quiet brass twist fastener.

With the exception of Ruger, all of the above firms can supply their black powder holsters with authentic, period-style matching belts. Red River's products are obtainable only by direct mail, but the others are sold through retail sporting goods stores. It might be a good idea to first send for catalogs of the firms that interest you and see what is available, as most dealers do not stock the entire line, but they can order a specific make and model for you. Delivery

Ruger's Practical Holster offers total gun protection as well as a silent twist-snap on the flap.

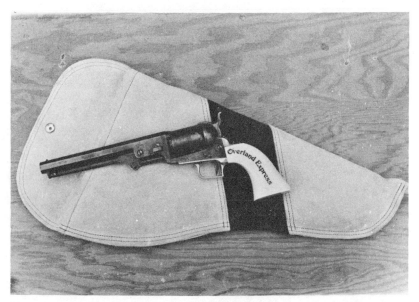

It's a fact of life that some hunting handguns are more valuable than others. Author's well-used Colt 1851 Navy re-issue was fitted with custom ivory Eagle grips by Art Jewel. When transporting such pieces, Uncle Mike's lined pistol case is a good investment for their continued protection. The case will fit even the biggest dragoon pistol.

usually takes a month from Lawrence, Bianchi, or Ruger to your dealer's store.

One nice feature of the flap holster is that it can be used to protect your revolver while transporting it to and from the hunt. However, nothing beats the plushly-lined black powder pistol case from Uncle Mike's, a cushioned, suede-covered protection that is large enough to encompass the bulkiest Dragoon. When checking in my black powder revolver on an airplane en route to an out-of-state hunt, I always store it in one of these cases after having it inspected and before locking it in my suitcase.

No gun should be stored in a holster or enclosed case for more than a few days, as moisture can condense and cause rust.

Single shot pistoleers have a slightly different problem when hunting, as no leather company mass produces holsters for their

Most trapper-era single shots come with traditional belt hooks, which eliminates the immediate need for a holster, but does little toward protecting the gun.

one-shots. The Green River Forge, CVA and Lyman users have a slight advantage with their belt hooks. Although convenient to carry over a short distance, these authentic devices still do not offer protection for the gun. Merely sticking the pistol in your belt is practically guaranteed to cause a clattering sound after a while, followed by a dull thud as the gun hits the ground, and then a string of profanity that usually echoes off the mountaintops for two or three minutes. A better system is to seek out one of the custom leather workers in your area, or drop a line to one of the clothing shops such as The Buffalo Robe or La Pelleterie telling them what style of pistol you have and asking for a quote on a leather crossdraw holster. It may also be possible to acquire an inexpensive used revolver holster and cut off the bottom so that your single shot can fit through. One of my first holsters for a brace of coach pistols was made that way back in the 1950's and I still use those holsters today. However, be sure to fasten a leather strap to fit around the grip or hammer to keep the gun in its place when not in use.

After all, if there is one thing a muzzleloading hunter should never lose, it is his ability to command extra firepower with one hand. It can mean the difference between lost game, or having extra meat on the table. Both are added benefits for the hunter who chooses to pack a pistol!

◀•▶

CHAPTER FIVE

MAKING YOUR FIRST (AND ONLY) SHOT COUNT

T he most beautifully-built rifle, a perfectly poured powder charge, the season's clearest day, and a Boone and Crockett buck standing broadside after just brushing against a day-glo orange painted fence, the color of which still clings to the fur over his heart/lung area, all won't mean a thing if the hunter is unable to place his one and only shot in exactly the right place, when and where he wants it. Yet, after more than two-and-a-half decades of hunting with black powder arms, I am continually amazed at the number of otherwise knowledgeable sportsmen who haul their newly acquired muzzleloaders out of the box, fire a few rounds with it to make sure the bullet is coming out of the front of the barrel, and then self-assuredly saunter off into the fields without ever really knowing where their rifle was hitting, or if it was hitting anything at all. I am not just referring to the first-time out pilgrim who is as yet unfamiliar with all the nuances of his chosen charcoal burner. For some obscure reason hidden deep in the psyche of "cartridge rifle" hunters, there is a tendency for a few of these sportsmen, weaned on the centerfire big game rifle, to forget all the rules when they shift their sights (figuratively speaking, unfortunately, not literally) to the muzzleloader. Perhaps it is because they sense the black powder rifle comes from a less complicated era in our hunting past. But surely anyone who has ever performed the mechanical task of shucking in a factory-assembled round and discharging this pre-ordained cartridge at a cross-haired reticle must sense the greater challenge and demands of the black powder rifle, the *ultimate* big game contender. But this *laissez faire* attitude towards marksmanship occasionally comes from our own ranks, too. There are more than just a few supposedly experienced black powder hunters who traditionally take the ol' smokepole out in back of the house each year before deer season opens, and fire a single blast at the woodpile, figuring that if they can hit a quarter cord of pine, then they

Here's proof that hair-splitting accuracy is possible for the hunter who practices. This buckskinner has just fired a lead ball at the cutting edge of an ax blade, splitting the ball in the center and breaking a clay "bird" on either side.

can surely knock down a big buck. After all, few big game animals are larger than a woodpile, right?

However, justice will prevail, for these are the same individuals who usually return home each season empty-handed, grumbling incoherently about "the one that got away," or pontificating in wonder about the legendary "Great Ghost Deer," whose mystical body permitted a carefully aimed Mini-ball to pass completely through it without ever leaving a mark!

It saddens me to hear an otherwise knowledgeable buckskinner, clutching an authentically fashioned long gun that is obviously a proud possession, lament, "Mah ol' smokepole kin shoot a fur piece better than Ah ever will." That type of self-effacing modesty has no place in the muzzleloading hunter's vocabulary, for simply translated, it means, "I have never taken the time to perfect my marksmanship skills, so that I can shoot as good as my gun will let me." Far from being admirable, this type of philosophy is blasphemy to an important part of our American heritage, an insult to a finely-made rifle, and a sacrilege to the art of black powder hunting. It is also foolhardy for the front-loading hunter not to develop his shooting skills, for unlike some other worthwhile muzzleloading re-enactments, this black powder hobby puts him in a real-life situation where he must pit his skills against those of a wild creature. Therefore, as a means of self-preservation, if not pride, the black powder sportsman's goal should be to build maximum confidence in his hunting skills and shooting ability.

Given the fine quality of black powder rifles available today, there is absolutely no reason the primitive hunter cannot develop the same marksmanship skills as his muzzleloading brother, the match shooter, for in both sports, accuracy is one of the primary ingredients for achieving success. The basics of muzzleloading marksmanship for the hunter involve the same principles as practiced with any firearm: proper sight picture, holding and "squeezing" off your shot, and — to a lesser extent — breathing. However, the ramrod-using hunter also has a few more variables thrown in that makes his sport a little more challenging. Loading is a critical factor that the self-contained metallic cartridge hunter doesn't necessarily have to worry about, but it can make the difference between a hit or a miss with a muzzleloader. The amount of powder poured down the bore,

Hunters in the field do not always have the time or luxury for carefully measuring out their powder, so the place to determine a proper load for your rifle is on the range, before hunting season opens.

the type of bullet used, and even the force with which it is rammed home upon the charge will all affect the point of impact at any given range. Additionally, the type of bullet used can mean the difference between an animal that is humanely harvested, or one that is only wounded and must be tracked and found before it can be shot again, causing an extra hardship for both hunter and quarry that could have been prevented.

Of course, learning to become a crack shot with your long rifle is not a guarantee that you will fill your tag each year, but it does cut down the odds a bit. If you do spot a legal animal and he is within shooting range, and you have practiced your marksmanship and loading skills, chances are pretty good that you will be skinning him out before the sun sets. The legends of such historic figures as Davy Crockett, Kit Carson, and Buffalo Bill Cody were all built upon the same practical working knowledge of correct sight alignment, trigger pull, and proper loading. Contrary to popular belief at the time, the shooting skills of these men were not inherited; they were learned by long hours of dedicated practice. There is no such thing as a "natural shot." To be sure, some individuals are blessed with steadier nerves than others, or have sharper vision, but anyone can acquire match-winning/game-getting accuracy with a hunting rifle if he will practice. One of the best percussion rifle shots I ever met was a Viet Nam veteran who was confined to a wheelchair. He had a Dixie Gun Works New Squirrel Rifle in .40 caliber fitted with double-set triggers. Everytime he would touch that replica long gun off, his chair would roll back a few feet from the recoil if he didn't lock the wheels, but he could place five shots in the same ragged hole at 50 yards, swabbing out the bore each time after he fired. Some other men standing on two legs and outfitted with more expensive rifles could never beat him. His secret? Practice; he was on that range every weekend, perfecting his shooting skills.

Considering the fact that the killing zone of most big game animals covers an area measuring over 8 inches in diameter, the natural question to ask is, why be concerned about ten-ring accuracy within this basketball-sized target? The answer is obvious: unlike the metallic cartridge hunter who can summon up repeat shots just as fast as he can work his bolt, lever, slide, or trigger finger, the muzzle-loading hunter is limited to one all-telling, all-knowing, ultimate shot. And chances are he will only get to fire it once each season, for when that smoke curtain lifts, it either goes up on an empty stage or a dead player. How that one shot is fired and where it hits is all that separates you from having a full freezer and a wonderful "war" story to tell and retell in front of that winter's fire.

For the small game hunter, the need for pin-point accuracy is readily apparent, for fur-bearing targets like rabbits, groundhogs and squirrels offer very little of themselves to aim at under the best of situations. But what about the big game hunter; is his ability to shoot ten-ring groups really necessary, considering the fact that he is firing a bullet that is at least a half-inch in diameter, and is sent thundering out the bore with enough black powder to make it crash through eight or more pine boards?

The answer to that question is that velocity and foot pounds of energy are only two-thirds of a three part solution to successful big game hunting; a lot depends on *where* your shot hits. With a muzzleloading rifle, there are only two sure-fire, instant game-dropping shots: the brain (ideal for meat-only animals, but a taxidermist's nightmare if you want your trophy mounted), and the spine, one of the most difficult to make and usually attributed to luck (although any primitive hunter worth his weight in beaver pelts is tradition-bound to refer to it as "skill" when it happens to him). Therefore, luck and skill notwithstanding, most hunters, myself included, traditionally aim for the heart/lung area, where a majority of a game animal's vitals are stored. However, even when lethally hit with a 400-grain-plus projectile, most big game animals will still run anywhere from a few feet to a hundred yards before dropping, and then may require a second shot to finish the job (another reason to get in the habit of instantly reloading your rifle after shooting, as we will discuss in Chapter Eight).

Placing your one shot in an 11 × 14 inch, picture-frame sized area, at 50 to 100 yards may seem simple enough while zeroing in on the firing line, but out in Nature's conservatory, it is quite a different story. For one thing, you will be "guesstimating" your range, as no pre-determined yardage markers will be set up. Additionally, chances are you will be out of breath, or hyperventilated with excitement, or both, making it even more difficult to hold "dead on," thus increasing the possibility of throwing your shot off a little from your point-of-aim. This entire "moment of truth" situation for

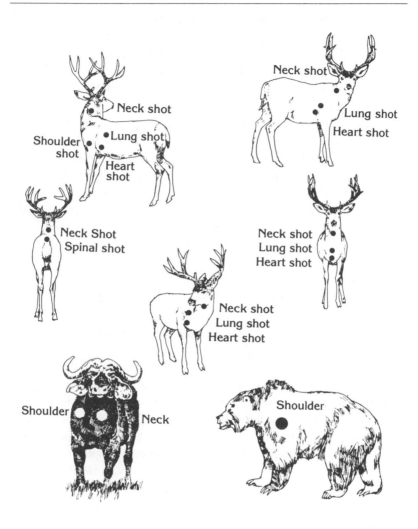

All the powder and lead you can stuff in your pockets won't do you any good unless you know where to place your shots. Before going out on a black powder hunt, study photographs of the game you're going after and learn where the vital spots are. Then practice your marksmanship, firing the same loads you'll be using on your hunt. If you fire and miss, you won't get a second opportunity, unless your quarry is deaf, dumb, or already dead! You *must* make your first shot count. You do this by having a rifle of sufficient quality and caliber, having it loaded correctly, steadying your nerves enough to squeeze off a shot exactly where you want it, and knowing where to shoot. These illustrations show you the best aiming spots with a muzzleloading rifle. Learn to memorize them before your next hunt. Illustrations courtesy of Browning Arms.

the black powder sportsman may be further complicated by the fact that many shooters having a favorite hunting arm that is rifled with a slow twist for the round ball prefer to shoot the more effective conical slug when after big game. Thus, a front-stuffer such as the Browning Mountain Rifle or Lyman Great Plains Rifle, both of which are capable of printing cloverleafs all day long when fed round balls, will normally open those groups up to at least 3 or 4 inches when their shooting diet is changed to conicals or Minis. This is no fault of the gun—it is simply a matter of rifling, which still places the bullet within the picture frame "killing zone," but with a wider variance, and hence, a greater margin for error on the hunter's part. All of these factors are reasons to have as much control of that all-important first shot as is skillfully and mechanically possible. Shooting too high or too low, chances are you'll either kick up dust or penetrate air; either way you will have spooked the only game you may see that day. If your shot is too far forward, you'll miss, or at best only wound your animal; shoot too far back and you may inflict a slow, lingering death on a gut-shot creature, unless you are able to quickly find and dispatch him with a second shot.

Tracking a wounded game animal is one of the most distasteful but necessary responsibilities a hunter will ever have to perform, not so much because of the extra hardship he must endure, but due to the throat-tightening thought that one of God's noble creatures is being made to suffer because of careless marksmanship. In addition to this mental and moral anguish, there is also the physical threat of danger. Hunting camps are rife with tales of attacks by lead-angered bears and cougars, but any game animal can be dangerous when wounded, even the docile deer. Many years ago on a hunt outside of Payson, Arizona, I came across a nimrod sitting on a rock and clutching his blood-soaked pants; his leg had been gored by a dying four-pointer that he had shot, and then approached with too little caution. It was the last act that the deer was able to perform, for his partially-gutted carcass lay just a few yards away. I managed to get the hunter back into town and patched up, but the memory of us following his own blood trail to pack out his deer the next day brought home the fact that those antlers were not originally intended to be hatracks. Col. Mike Powasnick of Trail Guns Armory tells a hair-raising story of tracking down a recordbook Cape Buffalo that had already absorbed two slugs from a Kodiak Double Rifle. Rather than follow the big bull's tracks, Mike wisely decided to crest a hill for a better view of the situation. It was lucky he did, for there, not more than ten yards away, was the giant animal, partially concealed by brush, watching his backtrail and waiting to charge. Two more close-range shots from Powasnick's .58 Kodiak put a spectacular end to this hunted-turned-hunter scenario. "It was one of the most exciting moments of my life," says Powasnick, in a classic understatement. But it does point out the crucial need for being able to place your shots exactly where you want them and using the utmost caution in the follow-up; you may not get a second chance.

Rifles like the Kodiak, Sharps, Thompson/Center Renegade, and the Sile Hawken Hunter have fast-twist rifling and are designed to shoot conical bullets. Thus, they will normally group tighter with these projectiles than guns with slower-twist lands and grooves like the Dixie Tennessee Mountain Rifle or the Mowrey Plains Rifle. These guns will shoot tightest with the patched round ball. But no matter which gun you choose, or what shape of soft-lead projectile you decide to ram down the bore, any quality muzzleloader can be made to shoot with deadly hunting accuracy if you will take the time to get to know your gun and perfect your marksmanship skills with it.

The first step for hunting marksmanship does not involve any shooting at all. It is simply taking the time to get acquainted with your black powder firearm. Like any partner that you want to take hunting with you, it pays to get to know your muzzleloader well. You want to make sure it will be able to withstand rugged conditions and will not let you down when you need it. If it is a gun that you already own, take it out and look it over with renewed interest and perhaps, more exacting criteria by which to judge its possible performance. If it is a rifle, are the sights suitable to the type of hunting you plan to do with it or should they be replaced? Is that front silver blade too thin to be seen clearly in dim light? If so, perhaps it should be substituted with a thicker hunting sight, like those made by Tedd Cash or The Hawken Shop. Is the trigger pull set where you want it, or should it be adjusted? Personally, I like 2½ pounds for a "set" trigger and 5 to 7 pounds unset. What about the lock?

Have you ever taken it out of the stock to clean off the fouling from last November's shoot? Could it use a light coating of non-gumming, non-freezing lubricant, such as Marble's or TufOil? Is the nipple becoming battered? Maybe it should be replaced, perhaps by one of the stainless steel Hot Shots, as discussed in Chapter Six. Is anything living or growing in the bore since the last time you cleaned it? Are all the screws and wedges tightly in place? These are the features that should be checked before *every* hunt. The great outdoors is no place to discover you've got a problem.

If you use a cap and ball revolver as a hunting sidekick, check out the timing to be sure that each chamber lines up correctly with the bore. Could the internal parts use a light coating of oil and perhaps a little fine tuning to produce smoother functioning?

So much for preventive maintenance on the gun you already own. If you are the lucky recipient of a newly-purchased muzzleloader, then you have an even more enjoyable pre-hunt task ahead of you, for one of the great untainted pleasures for the muzzleloading hunter in today's world is that magic moment when he unpacks his rifle for the first time. Like any hunting partner which you are meeting for the first time, it is important that you get well ac-

Hunting sights on some rifles may be improved by the addition of products such as these: *Left to right*, the Tedd Cash silver blade front sight, CVA front and rear adjustable sight combination, and Marble's adjustable buckhorn rear sight, normally associated with lever-actions "ca'tridge guns," but just as practical on muzzleloaders.

quainted with your new muzzleloader; learn the stuff it is made of, how it is put together, and how well it will perform in an emergency. Take your muzzleloader out of the box and look it over carefully, for familiarization breeds confidence and is the first step towards becoming a good shot. Most half-stock plains-type rifles will be broken down into the barrel and stock sections; Kentuckies and other long rifles will be in one piece, their barrels forever fastened to the stock with pins, which are not normally meant to be removed.

Some manufacturers, such as Thompson/Center and Lyman include extremely comprehensive and detailed booklets with their guns, giving its history, details on its safe operation, and suggestions as to proper loading. Personally, I wish this procedure would be followed by every black powder manufacturer, for it helps promote responsibility, safety, and enjoyment for the shooter.

New guns are usually heavily covered with grease, so carefully unwrap them and lay them on some newspaper. If there is any literature, the next step is to read the enclosed folders, guarantees, etc., from cover to cover. I read everything at least twice to make up for the folks who never read them once. The gun should be completely degreased, preferably outside of the house to keep peace with those of the opposite sex. That brown colored goop may be fine for preventing rust from the factory, but it can clog flash-holes and gum up your lock work. Use a hefty supply of paper towels, old rags and occasional moistening with commercial black powder solvents such as Hoppe's No. 9 or Hodgdon's Spit-Bath. Don't forget to take out and clean the nipple on percussion arms and use a vent-pick or piece of wire to clean out the touch-hole on flintlocks. The next step is to swab the bore; on guns with browned barrels, you will probably pull out a hideously rusty patch, so it is good to leave a light coating of oil down the tube to protect the rifling until the gun is fired. The first shot will usually burn out the rest of the loose discoloration.

For rifles and single shot pistols, using a properly fitting screwdriver to guard against premature scratches and burrs, carefully loosen the screws holding the lock in place and back them out part way. With a plastic or leather hammer, gently tap the screws from the left side toward the lock to loosen it from the stock. A "gentle" forcing is what is needed, for many locks are closely inletted to the stock and care must be taken to prevent the wood around the lock from splintering.

Once the lock is removed, study its inner workings and function; psychologically, the more you know about your gun, the better you'll shoot with it. This is also a good time to carefully inspect the lock for cracked or broken springs (yes, it does occasionally happen, but practically all reliable manufacturers will replace them without cost if the gun is new). Thoroughly degrease the lock and lightly oil it with a non-freezing lubricant. Place a few drops of oil on the trigger mechanism also. Don't forget to wipe off the ramrod and to degrease and inspect the front and rear sights on the barrel; it is exasperating to have drifting bits of dirt and wayward bugs clinging to a grease-coated sight when you are trying to zero in your thunderstick on the range, to say nothing of firing it on the hunt.

This also is an ideal time to rub one or two coats of linseed oil into the stock to give it a misty sheen and help protect it from possible exposure to rain and snow later in the year. Do not use ultraquick commercially prepared synthetic coatings on your hunting rifle. They impart an unnaturally shiny, light-reflective finish to your wooden stock that can spook game and make the natural composition of your wood seem out-of-place in a wilderness setting. We are not talking about esthetics in this case, but rather how to keep your rifle from being easily detected by wildlife. Glossy polymer and resin finishes may be fine for a showcased rifle on display, but they have no place on a muzzleloading hunting gun. On the other hand, nothing looks as natural as a few coats of linseed oil hand-rubbed into a stock, especially when this ritual has been followed for a few seasons. It also aids in bringing out the natural wood grain of your rifle. Do not apply the linseed in heavy doses, but rub it into the wood with your hand for about five minutes, then wipe off the excess amount with a paper towel, and let the stock stand in a corner overnight. Repeat the procedure once more the next day, and you will have a stock that will be able to withstand the elements. That is not to say your gunstock will be sealed and completely waterproof, for the wood must still "breathe" to prevent cracking. But at least it will be protected and after a few seasons of this treatment, will begin to develop a deep, rich luster that is impossible to obtain with most of the synthetic "easy-on" solutions.

Unlike rifles, black powder revolvers usually come from the factory completely assembled, but are usually packed in enough grease to keep a four-wheel drive vehicle skidding nonstop from Bangor, Maine to Los Angeles, California. The cylinder, bore, and frame should be completely wiped down and oiled, with special attention paid to the chambers and nipple flash holes. Too much oil or grease in these areas will contaminate your powder and can prevent the flash of even a Hot Cap from reaching your charge.

At this point, it is always a good idea to double check the tightness of all screws, the secureness of the sights, and to make sure that there are no burrs or dings on the muzzle to mar accuracy. You should also be sure that your bore is adequately rifled. As far-fetched as it may sound, I once received a frantic request from an experienced black powder shooter who could not get his 1860 Army to group any tighter than 10 inches at 50 feet. A cursory inspection of the gun immediately revealed the problem: the bore had never been rifled! Of course, it would have been ideal for packing the cylinders full of No. 6 shot and using it as a snake gun, but this was not his original intention. So back to the factory it went, although looking at the incident with crystal clear hindsight, I think that replica smoothbore would have had more value today as a collector's variation. Nonetheless, the point is that manufacturing errors can occur, even from the best of companies, so check your new gun carefully at home, in order to avoid a mechanically-caused disappointment on your hunt, when you are far from replaceable parts. For the black powder hunter, there is no such thing as being too careful or too cautious.

With your muzzleloader oiled and re-assembled, the next step is to take it out to the shooting range. Actually, any open area providing a safe backdrop and known distances up to 100 yards is satisfactory, as long as it is legal to shoot there. When sighting in a hunting rifle, you will be using far more equipment than you would normally pack in the field. But for the loading process, I try to only use those implements that I plan to carry with me on an actual hunt. The reasons are twofold: first, the more practical experience you get with your hunting "possibles," the faster and easier it will be for you to reload in the field, and second, if you need to replace or increase the black powder items you plan to use for hunting, it is better to discover this fact near civilization, rather than in the woods on that once-a-year big game hunt. For the same reason, range shooting is also a good time to test out that new powder measure or "improved" capper you just bought.

Basically, the items you should take to the range are:

1. At least one can of the proper granulation of black powder or Pyrodex. (When shooting hunting loads of 100-plus grains, it is surprisingly easy to go through a can in a half-day. During one field test for a .58 rifle which required an unusual amount of sight adjustment, I burned up two cans of FFG in one shooting session and had to return for more before the gun was properly zeroed in.)

2. A tin of caps or extra flints, depending on the ignition system you are shooting.

3. Plenty of cleaning patches or rags for swabbing out the bore of your gun.

Familiarization with your new cap and ball begins on a shooting range, not on the hunting range, where excitement can prove to be a distraction.

4. A good quality black powder cleaning solvent, such as CVA Old Time Bore Cleaner, Hodgdon's Spit-Bath, or The Hawken Shop's Ol' Griz.

5. Cleaning rod or ramrod with cleaning jag.

6. Fifty pure lead Minis, Maxis or round balls, depending on what you have decided to shoot. I usually take some of each to see which will perform best in my gun, although I have a definite preference for the conical shaped bullet for big game hunting, even with slow twist rifling.

7. Lubricant (and patching material and patch knife if you are shooting round balls).

8. Short-starter.

9. Leather- or plastic-headed hammer for drifting fixed sight rifles.

10. Two or three screwdrivers of various sizes for adjustable sights or making minor repairs.

11. Powder measure.

12. Nipple wrench and pick.

13. At least ten standard NRA-type 100-yard targets.

14. Swiss files for shaping fixed rear sights and lowering front sights on fixed sight rifles.

15. Masking tape or thumbtacks for affixing your target to a board or support.

Revolver shooters should also take along some Crisco, black powder grease, or chemically treated wads to seal off the chambers, thus preventing the rather spectacular phenomenon known as multiple discharge. You might also wish to take along paper and pencil for making notes, and a spotting scope or binoculars to cut down the number of treks you'll be making downrange to check your targets. Tin can plinking doesn't make it; you need paper targets to see where you are hitting in order to properly zero in your rifle for hunting season. If you are not shooting at a regular range, one of the

[149]

inexpensive portable target stands sold by Dixie Gun Works is helpful for mounting your targets. As a final suggestion, you may want to pack a bedroll or a couple of blankets for rolling up to help steady your rifle if no bench rest is available, and you must shoot while sitting or lying on the ground.

Naturally, when firing any muzzleloading gun—percussion or flintlock, rifle, or pistol—shooting glasses are an absolute *must*, unless, of course, you feel that you no longer have a need for depth perception. Hot gases, airborne particles of burning powder, and flying cap fragments or pieces of flint all could cause irreparable damage should they come in contact with your eyes. Even in the field, many black powder hunters that I know wear tinted shooting glasses to protect their vision and help cut the glare. Yellow is normally the best color for defining contrast, but I prefer gray or brown as a compromise between clarity and glare reduction.

Although not as mandatory for the black powder shooter, ear muffs or individually inserted ear plugs are also a good idea. However, ear protection should be required wearing apparel when shooting your muzzleloader on a gun range alongside those big, door-busting, modern-day smokeless powder magnums. In this case, I highly recommend ear muffs, not plugs, which do little to protect the sound-sensitive area of the entire ear from those booming shock waves. The report of a muzzleloader is not as deafening as the smokeless powder guns, but over a period of time, it, too, can be damaging. The danger lies in the fact that you never know your hearing is fading until it is too late. Being your basic worrier, I began stuffing cotton in my ears when I first began shooting in the early 1950's. (The sporting goods stores didn't carry bona fide "hearing protection" in those days.) Oh, I took my share of ribbing about it. (Hey, kid, you trying to keep something from falling out or getting in?) But today, my hearing is unimpaired, while I cannot say the same for many of my gun-shooting and gun-writing contemporaries. So start at the beginning and you will have a better chance of hearing that faint rustle of leaves or snap of a twig that could signal your game's presence. Unlike eye protection, however, ear plugs or muffs should not be worn while hunting, as it will interfere with your ability to detect game. Besides, the only shot you will hopefully hear all day will be your own.

This is the correct offhand position from which most hunting shots are fired. Note left arm is tucked in to help steady long or heavy barrels; right arm is parallel to ground to avoid canting rifle, which will throw your shot off.

When firing heavy-duty hunting loads in a new gun for the first time, I always wear a medium-weight, long sleeve shooting coat or shirt, and occasionally a pair of light leather gloves, to protect my arms and hands from the unknown blast. Uncle Mike's Hot Shot nipples can alleviate some of this apprehension, but I still carry a small scar on my wrist, left by a flying cap fragment that was launched by 110 grains of FFG behind a .58 Mini-Ball in a new rifle. As I said before, you cannot be too careful. Once your hunting load has been

[151]

proven and found safe, the gloves and the arm protection can be dispensed with if you wish, but leave your eye and ear protection on as long as there is a trigger to be pulled during the range testing process.

Like the target shooter, the muzzleloading hunter must be thoroughly familiar with the basics of marksmanship before he can adequately zero in his rifle for game. The elements include the following:

1. Firing position. For the hunter, this will normally involve standing and sitting, both of which are illustrated in this chapter. The muzzleloading hunter should also take advantage of any type of steadying rest he can, such as a fence post, or tree limb. It is best to cushion your rifle with your hand, but in any case, never let the barrel directly touch your rest; the vibration of the shot will cause the barrel to move before the bullet leaves the muzzle, resulting in a shot that misses its mark.

2. Trigger pull. The trigger finger should squeeze, not yank, the trigger. Otherwise you will jerk your shot, which will throw you off target. For maximum control, it is best to pull the trigger with the fleshy part of your finger, not with the joint. If your shot is unhurried, you can use the set trigger for improved shot placement. Do not use it in a hurried or tension-filled hunting situation as the gun could prematurely go off.

3. Breathing. This is something we all do unconsciously, but controlled breathing can help steady your nerves and your shot. Take a deep breath, let half of it out, fire and expel the rest of the air in your lungs. That slight pause will steady your body motions, thereby aiding your shot placement. It also helps control your aim should you come upon your game when you are out of breath (a frequent occurrence with hunters, due to strenuous chase or high altitudes).

4. Sight picture. No matter what type of sights you use, fixed or adjustable, they should be calibrated to hit at point-of-aim. That is, when the front sight is centered in between the notch of the rear sight, the bullet will strike at a point that is directly in line with the top of the front sight.

We are now ready to zero in our gun. But before that can happen, two questions have to be answered: What hunting load will be used, and what range should we zero in for? The answers depend upon what rifle/powder/ball combination we are using and what type of game we are hunting.

Today's black powder hunter can pick from three of the most popular bullets: the traditional round ball, the Civil War-inspired Mini-Ball, or the recently-created Maxi-Ball. All three have their good and bad points. The round ball, the choice of most buckskinners and traditionalists, normally exhibits greater accuracy than Minis or Maxis, but is ballistically less efficient. The Minis and Maxis, on the other hand, are not always as accurate (2-inch groups at 50 yards and up to 6-inch groups at 100 yards are about average, and more than adequate for the big game hunter), but contain far more lead and possess greater killing (shock) power on deer-sized and larger game.

Some slow-twist rifles are superbly accurate up to 100 yards. But they lack killing power for most big game animals. That is not to say a round ball cannot kill a deer or bear or moose, but to do the job requires more powder than what would be used with a conical slug to achieve the same striking energy, which is what a hunter is chiefly concerned with, not muzzle velocity. The following chart shows the differences between a conical and round ball, using the three most popular big game calibers:

	.50 with 90 grains FFFG Conical/ Round Ball		.54 with 100 grains FFFG Conical/ Round Ball		.58 with 110 grains FFG Conical/ Round Ball	
Bullet Weight (in grains)	370	180	410	220	505	260
Muzzle Velocity (fps)	1,377	1,686	1,374	1,662	1,136	1,314
Muzzle Energy (ft. lbs)	1,556	1,135	1,716	1,347	1,445	995
Striking Energy at 100 yards	775	396	1,044	515	1,051	463

To compute how your hunting rifle will perform with a specific powder and projectile combination, I highly recommend the *Lyman Black Powder Handbook*, an excellent reference that depicts all popular loads in all popular calibers. But from the abbreviated illustration given above, it is obvious that the conical bullet, through its greater weight and striking force, is the better projectile for big or dangerous game.

For small game, I opt for the round ball, as its greater velocity and lighter weight make it extremely flat-shooting (compared with the "rainbow" trajectory of the conicals) and accurate well beyond 100 yards, although most of your shooting will be done at shorter ranges. And of course, the round ball's smaller size gives it definite superiority when used on small game, as less meat is destroyed.

As for the Maxis, I use them occasionally for a first shot, but find them too hard to start down the muzzle (the top rib must actually be pushed into the rifling to give it its spin when fired) and thus, find them impractical for any hunter needing to reload in a hurry. I much prefer a pre-greased Mini, which can be rammed down the bore more easily.

Even though rifles with slower-twist barrels (i.e., one in 60 inches) will handle a round ball better than a Mini or Maxi, which perform best with faster twists (such as one in 48 inches), there are exceptions. Even with today's mass-produced muzzleloaders, every gun is still a law unto itself. For example, one of my favorite hunting guns is a custom-made Hawken with a Sharon one-in-66-inches twist. It is an accepted black powder axiom that this gun will shoot round balls accurately but would fail to pass the 50-yard test with a Mini. But, during one memorable testing session, I discovered that my Hawken, when loaded with 75 grains of FFG and a Mini, shot identical groups as it did with my standard hunting charge of 120 grains of FFG and a patched round ball. This is contrary to everything that is ballistically known in the black powder field, but it is a verified fact, at least with my particular rifle. Normally, shooting conical bullets in a fast twist barrel (which I often do) opens the group up to 4 to 6 inches at 50 yards, severely limiting your range, but giving you far greater killing power. A nice trade-off, I think. However, your rifle might shoot differently, or the same or even better. The point is, you will never know until you spend

some time on the range with your rifle, powder, and bullets, experimenting with a multitude of combinations to find the right hunting
load for your chosen muzzleloader. The ultimate goal is to achieve
an even balance between accuracy and power.

Even when you have finally zeroed your front-stuffer to shoot
dead center with a fixed hunting load, there will be situations in
which you may have to employ "Kentucky windage." This legendary shooting practice is nothing more than holding slightly off of
your target, either left or right, high or low, to compensate for some
uncontrollable factor, such as a hard-blowing wind or fast-running
game. Shotgunners like to refer to it as leading their target, but it is
"Kentucky windage" just the same. All it takes is a little practice
and a lot of luck.

I zero all my hunting loads to hit dead-on at 50 yards. I then fire
these same loads at 100-yard targets and mentally record where
they hit. For example, I know that with my "75 grains of FFG plus
Mini-Ball" formula, when used in specific .54 rifles, I shoot 2 inches
low at 100 yards. Thus, I am confident of my ability to place lethal
shots on deer within these boundaries. Although a muzzleloader
can kill well beyond the 100-yard limit, most shooters do not have the
eyesight or holding ability with open sights to place clean-killing
shots beyond that distance. But don't feel you're letting the "big ones"
get away; practically all of my black powder kills have been within 75
yards. The longest shot I ever took was at 125 yards, and that was
only because the grandest elk I had ever seen was rapidly moving
out of range of my Sharps. Sure, you could scope your charcoal-
burner to get more range and accuracy, although some states such
as Washington, prohibit this practice during hunting season. But
in that case, you would not be taking advantage of the black powder
challenge, and not reaping the full romance of the hunt or the pride
of the kill.

For dropping even small-sized deer at any range, I would not
recommend a powder charge of *less* than 65 grains of FFG, although
most of your big game hunting loads will fall in the 75- to 120-grain
range for conical or patched ball. Small game rifles will usually be
between 20 and 40 grains of FFG. Once you get a hunting load you
are satisfied with, stick with it and learn what it can do at all ranges.
Never vary your hunting load in the field or your point of impact

could change, resulting in a missed shot. And it can't be said too often: **Never use anything other than black powder or Pyrodex** in your front-stuffer. Today's guns are well-made, but their barrels and breeches and your head and hands will not take *any* load of smokeless powder. So keep it safe; black powder or Pyrodex *only*. Pyrodex RS can be used for all rifle calibers. If you prefer black powder, I recommend FFFG for calibers up to .50 and FFG for .54's and larger. FFFFG is extremely fine grained, produces higher pressures and should *only* be used for priming flintlocks. But if you forget your priming flask all is not lost, for I have successfully primed with FFFG and FFG, although your flintlock may not be as sure-fire with the larger grains. Because of its chemical make-up, Pyrodex cannot be used in a flintlock; the priming charge does not generate enough heat to ignite the Pyrodex main charge.

When zeroing in your muzzleloader, you will save a lot of time and aggravation by cleaning out the bore between shots. Otherwise your point of impact will change with each pull of the trigger, even though your powder charge and sight picture are constant. The reason for this is the gradual build-up of black powder fouling, which

The *only* propellants to use in any muzzleloader: Pyrodex or black powder.

All hunting rifles should be bench-rested for initial zeroing in. Swab out bore between shots for best accuracy.

will increase internal pressures slightly and throw the bullet off from the previous shot. The more powder you use, or the smaller the caliber, the greater the fouling and the more effect it has upon your rifle. This situation can be reduced to some extent through the use of Pyrodex, which has slightly less fouling than black powder, but there is still enough variance to recommend running a wet patch and then a dry one down the bore between shots for maximum accuracy readings. I usually fire a three-shot group, as more than that puts more tension on you and creates a greater possibility of shooter error, such as flinching, which will affect your test group.

In working up a hunting load, you should be aware of the fact that too much powder can be as ineffective as too little. Not only may accuracy suffer, but with some guns, 100 grains of FFG can cause a Mini-Ball to strip right out of the rifling, resulting in a keyhole shot. I have encountered this phenomenon in a number of guns with shallow rifling (although the gain-twist rifling of the Enfield Muskatoon seems to avoid this), and was only able to solve the problem by switching to a flat-based conical, such as the paper-patched bullets put out by Shiloh Sharps, and the Lee R.E.A.L.

(Rifling Engraved At Loading) bullet, a unique compromise between the Maxi and the Mini. If you want to cast your own flat-based bullets, both Lee and Lyman carry the moulds.

Casting round balls for hunting requires extra quality control on your part, for bullet symmetry can affect your rifle's accuracy. Personally, I prefer to shoot pre-cast swaged round balls from CCI and Hornady. These balls are perfectly round and there is no sprue to worry about centering on the patch (otherwise the ball will deform in loading and you will have a "flyer" on your hands — or rather, somewhere in the air).

Consistency is the key to accuracy for any black powder shooter. For the hunter, that means once you have established your hunting load, always use the same pre-measured charges of powder, the same weight of bullet and even the same brand of caps. It may sound a little extreme, but I even use the same brand of lube on my Minis! And always ram the charge home with the same degree of force; never vary it or your shot may change its point of impact.

There is a reason for all this caution: We are eliminating as many of the variables as possible in order to allow for those factors

Always ram ball down firmly onto powder charge, but do not pound it hard enough to deform the lead, which will affect accuracy. Hold the ramrod close to the muzzle to avoid breakage.

beyond which we have no control. The main culprit in the field is weather, specifically temperature and humidity. Hot weather will make your powder burn quicker, and with more pressure than when hunting on cold days. Moisture can effect the combustionable spontaneity of your charge (another reason for priming the nipple and other aids which we will discuss in the next chapter). If you zero in your smokepole on the Black Canyon Range in Phoenix, Arizona and then take it to Rifle, Colorado on a deer hunt, it will shoot harder and about 2 inches higher in that loftier atmosphere. Still, none of these variances are enough to take you out of that 8-inch big game killing zone as long as you stay within the practical 100-yard range of your gun. Remember, the greater the distance, the greater the degree of variance. And never forget that a muzzleloading rifle can be as individualistic as the person shooting it!

It is important for the hunter to realize that not all hunting rifles are capable of pinpoint accuracy. My TVA Squirrel rifle can put three balls in the same ragged hole (ask me how I know, go ahead, ask me), yet I cannot get my Lyman Great Plains Rifle to group tighter than 2 inches. But both guns are superb rifles for the hunter, capable of taking any game that their range and calibers permit. The crucial factor is for the hunter to place his shot exactly in the vital area of the animal he is hunting. That means before going on your next hunt, study the anatomy of your game animal. Cut out photographs from the various outdoors magazines (you will rarely get a broadside shot, so "plan your angles," so to speak). NRA members may send to their Hunter Information Service and obtain cut-away views of various game animals. Study the heart, lung, brain, and spine areas and mark them in color. Commit them to memory.

On one of my many fabled bear hunts, I had pictures of black bear pasted to the refrigerator, my desk lamp, and my car's dashboard. People began to think I was some kind of bear pervert. My wife even suggested we have bear placemats made, but quickly withdrew her tongue-in-cheek offer when I began to look around for fur-covered silverware.

It is true the muzzleloading hunter may only have one shot, but if he does his pre-hunt shooting and planning correctly, that one shot may be all he'll need.

CHAPTER SIX

HUNTER'S HELPERS

F rom a practical point of view, all an experienced hunter needs is a properly loaded gun, some extra powder and lead, and a knife in order to pursue his hobby. However, the realities of the sport are such that, as soon as we are physically and financially able, most of us will embark upon a pleasant and dedicated search for additional shooting paraphernalia and related items, which we will continue to add to our plunder for the rest of our natural lives. The items thus acquired range from the most necessary (i.e., a better rifle or "hotter" cap), to basic "possibles" (such as an unbreakable ramrod or sharper patchknife), to down-right, fun-to-find "foofaraw" (a beaded pipebag or specially-tooled holster complete with your initials and a hand-dyed carving of your wife or girlfriend). All of these items are personally rewarding to own and instill an even deeper pride in the muzzleloading hunter. Also, they can also help make him more effective in the field.

It is difficult to say which additional items should be acquired first. Ideally, a hunter should get the best equipment he can afford, but on rare occasions this rule does not hold true. For example, my very first black powder hunting knife was a custom-crafted Bowie that I designed, and then had made for me by Nelson Cooper. It was the first knife he built after settling in California, and he dubbed it the Hacker California Bowie. It was a massive affair, capable of withstanding the severest treatment without losing its edge. How-ever, it often struck me as being too pretty to use and after a few years had passed, it assumed a somewhat embarrassing collector's status, wherein people began offering me more money for it than I thought made sense. So I retired the knife and now only wear it at rendezvous and other festive gatherings, opting to use my Randall or Green River knives (as the mood strikes me) for hunts.

It is safe to say that you should buy what you like, but in no in-stance should you sacrifice quality. Part of the challenge and fun of being a muzzleloading hunter is experimenting with new products, but try to examine them first to avoid the danger of adding cheap or unsafe items to your shooting box. Poorly-made items will only taint your image and detract from the hunting skills you already have. The products listed in this chapter are ones that I have personally used and I recommend them highly. But there are others coming to our attention every day, and this is not intended to be a complete

For hunters who are pipe smokers, La Pelleterie's Gage d'Amour holds an evening's worth of tobacco and a clay pipe. Clay pipes are available from The Tinder Box and most muzzleloading suppliers. The Gage d'Amour is hung in the lodge or worn around the neck in the hunter's camp, and is not for field use.

Six top quality knives for the hunter *(left to right)* Buck Trapper with skinning blade (for small game), the Navy Arms Green River, the Browning "Trailing Point" sheath knife, the Navy Arms English Bowie, the standard "Green River" blade by Case and Russell, and the Buck Frontiersman. For heavy-duty work, sheath knives are stronger than pocket knives, due to their sturdier construction. They are also more traditional.

listing of everything the black powder sportsman may need, although it certainly is a good start.

One of the few black powder accoutrements conspicuously absent in this book is the time-honored powder horn. Hanging next to my squirrel gun on my den wall, or simply viewed as a finely-crafted work of art, the powder horn has few equals for nostalgic beauty and charm. But in the hunter's camp, it has no practical place; I have never felt comfortable with a half-pound of black powder banging around at my side all day, somewhat like a small nineteenth century grenade waiting for the right moment to go off. Moreover, it dangles awkwardly under my arm, gets in the way when snap shooting, and, as most powder horns are handcrafted things of beauty, runs the risk of becoming damaged during the rigors of the hunt. It also slows down loading time, as first the powder must be poured from the horn into a measure, and then into the bore. Anyone who loads directly from his powder horn ought to have his head blown off, which is probably what will eventually happen. A glowing spark from a preceding shot, hidden in the dark recesses of your barrel, can ignite your next charge and turn your

[163]

Three of my knives *(from right)*; Cooper's Hacker California Bowie (since retired from active hunting service), Randall knife with stag handle, and "Green River" style blade.

powder horn into Gabriel's Horn! That is why I load only from pre-measured charges. The worst that can happen is a burnt hand and a face full of smoke. And you get to keep your head!

I must admit that, in my earlier years of hunting, I took quite a bit of ribbing over my use of pre-measured charges, the main comment being that it was not "right" for the black powder period. I think there were some references to my mental aptitude, also. But I persisted, firmly believing that the safe way was the best way. And then, one glorious day, while reading through the complete diary of the Lewis and Clark expedition for an article I was writing, I dis-

A good camp ax is indispensable, whether for chopping kindling or for splitting the breastbone of a buck. Although many are on the market, these three represent the best of the modern, primitive, and in-between. On the left is the Buck No. 106 Hunter's Ax, a superb twentieth century descendant of the eighteenth century tomahawk. It comes with a heavy-duty leather belt sheath. In the middle is TVA's quality replica of an original 'hawk. The hand-forged head must be firmly driven into the handle, then a wedge put in to help ensure the safety of the weapon. Basically designed as a throwing tool, it can be transformed into a handy and authentic camp utensil. On the right is the Hawken Shop "Head-Lok" Hawk, a unique blend of old and new. The head is firmly affixed to the handle by a screw. Two handle lengths are available, and a solid steel "pipe bowl" attachment is perfect for pounding tent pegs. A word of caution: Tomahawks were originally designed as weapons and should be treated with the same respect as your rifle.

The Hawken Shop makes a number of unique items that seem designed specifically for the hunter. One of them is their three-in-one Nipple Wrench, a compact 3½-inch rod which breaks down into a nipple wrench for pistol *or* rifle, and also serves as a screwdriver, nipple pick. Sounds more like a four-in-one tool to me.

covered that pre-measured charges were used by the famous Corps of Discovery way back in 1802! It seems that Captains Lewis and Clark felt they were not only safer, but insured the preservation of at least some of their precious black powder supply should their boats become swamped. Additionally, Lewis and Clark's pre-measured powder proved to be an ideal inventoried means of insuring that their hunters, often separated from the main party for days, would have sufficient ammunition to survive. Of course, pre-measured charges of sorts were also used in the form of paper cartridges during the Revolutionary War, and later, among the Sharps-carrying buffalo hunters of the Far West.

But putting history aside, the simple facts are that pre-measured charges are quicker, more convenient, and safer for the muzzleloading hunter to use, especially when one must reload under pressure for a fast second shot. Because the powder has been carefully measured out the day before the hunt, there is less chance of pouring in too much or too little when loading. In addition, rather than pour powder from horn to measure to gun, the charge is simply dumped straight down the bore. Less exposure means less chance of powder loss and danger from premature ignition, and less time spent in getting off that second shot.

Pre-measured charges may be carried in a variety of ways, the most economical being in those plastic black-and-gray cans that 35mm film comes in. You can usually obtain these waterproof containers free, just by asking for them at your local photography store. The only drawback to using the film cans is that their openings are rather large and can make it difficult to pour powder into a half-inch bore. As an improved method, for years I used small cardboard tubes, obtainable from Dixie Gun Works, which are sealed on one end and have a removable paper cap on the other. These tubes are very inexpensive and I still have not used up the supply I bought many moons ago. Unfortunately, they are not waterproof. Winchester Sutler makes a unique plastic tube that carries powder and

The four types of pre-measured black powder charges most readily available to today's shooters *(left to right)*: Butler Creek's Speed Loader, Dixie Gun Works "Quick Load" cardboard tubes, Muzzle Loaders "Speed Shell" (sold by Dixie), and 35mm film container. All work well, although the Butler Creek Speed Loader is the most practical, while the empty film can is the least expensive.

ball for a variety of calibers and can also be used for shotguns. However, on practically all of my hunts over the past few years, I have been using the rather excellent Quick Loaders, manufactured by Butler Creek. They are probably the most practical device of their type for the hunter. One end of the plastic Quick Loader tube holds up to two hundred grains of powder (more than most of us will ever fire in a single charge) and the other end has a compartment large enough for a greased .54 Mini-Ball. Both ends are sealed with a waterproof plastic lid, each of which has a built-in compartment for storing an extra No. 11 percussion cap. Flintlock shooters can carry patch and ball separately, using one end of the Quick Loader for the main charge and the other for the priming charge. A package of three comes with an optional black plastic belt clip, although I prefer carrying the Quick Loaders in my pocket or possibles bag, where there is less chance of losing them. They are one of the best investments a muzzleloading hunter can make.

I mentioned a possibles bag in the preceding paragraph, and this historic item of black powder apparel is definitely worthy of discussion, for it is somewhat of a paradox. Like the powder horn,

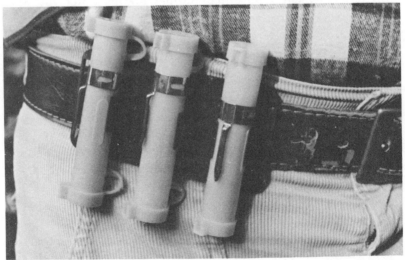

Butler Creek's Speed Loaders are available with handy, three-charge belt clip, although author has found they are easier to get at when carried loose in pocket or possibles bag.

Loading from Butler Creek's Speed Loader is quick and foolproof. Here, a pre-measured charge is poured down barrel; the other end of loader holds pre-greased conical bullet.

it is traditionally thought of in connection with muzzleloaders, but also like the horn, it shares some of the same pitfalls. It often bangs and swings at a hunter's side like a deranged prizefighter, and when some poor nimrod finds himself hot-footing it through brushy thickets and brambles, the possibles bag can grab onto a branch and dump its contents out on the ground as if it had a mind of its own. It only takes just a few such experiences to convince the hunter that there must be other methods of transporting his paraphernalia, and there are. As mentioned in Chapter Seven, my favorite solution is the bush coat, which is discussed on those pages in detail. However, the possibles bag does have its place on a muzzleloading hunt, although it is definitely not meant to go on long stalks or for action-packed game-getting, such as elk hunting on foot when much running must be done. But for hunting on horseback and for the still hunter, the possibles bag serves its purpose adequately, and it does ease the conscience of hunters who feel they must stick with tradition, no matter what the outcome.

Of the ready-made possibles bags on the market, the most

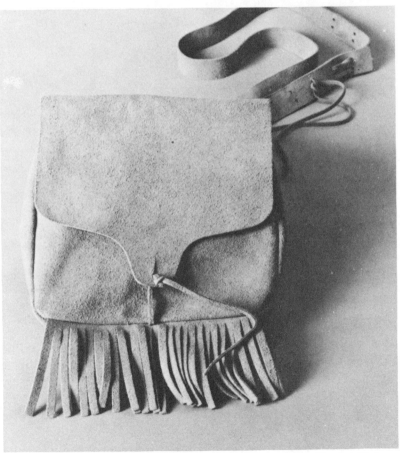

A good quality, ready-made possibles bag is this model by Uncle Mike's.

Two of my shooting bags; Plains Indian, on the left, and the Hivernant on the right. In the middle is Chahokia Sheath, trimmed in trade wood and beaded. It was made for TVA's Hudson Bay Knife by La Pelleterie.

easily obtainable for the hunter looking for quality at an affordable price are the half-dozen or so different styles carried by Dixie Gun Works (you'll have to get their present catalog to see what is currently available). There is also the nicely fashioned version by Uncle Mike's, which features an adjustable leather strap, leather tiedown thong for the flap, and a wide inner pocket and leather loops for keeping small items, such as capper and powder measure, within easy reach.

The hunter desiring a possibles bag with a more individualized custom look, such as beading, special compartments or extra fringe will have to seek out some of the numerous black powder dealers and craftsmen that abound throughout our nation—fortunately for us. Some of these shops and craftsmen can be found listed in Chapter Ten, but more will be discovered by leafing through the ads of some of the monthly black powder magazines such as *Muzzle Blasts* and *The Buckskin Report*.

For my own use, I wear a possibles bag when hunting on horseback and whenever I know there will not be much walking to do, such as going after squirrels. My long-time favorite bag is a leather and felt 1840's version made for me years ago by The Buffalo Robe in Reseda, California. That particular model is called the Hivernant and is pictured in this chapter. Depicted alongside the Hivernant is a Plains Indian Shooting Bag I recently ordered from La Pelleterie de Fort de Chartres. It is hand-sewn from a Hudson's Bay Blanket, is 100 percent authentic in design, and is extremely economical, although the beading around the sides and on the front will cost extra (I guess that places it under "foofaraw," although the bag itself is a "possibles"). Both bags are available in kit form for a few dollars less. You may wish to send for the catalogs of these firms — along with others you may find — to see what other styles they are now making. But a word of caution: It has been my experience that when having any black powder item handmade, be it shooting bag, moccasins or knife sheath, plan on it taking twice

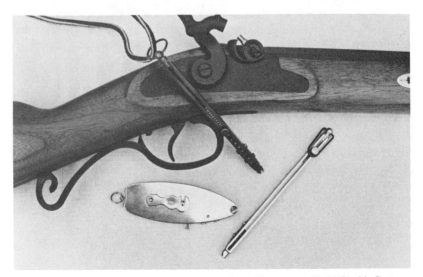

Two basic versions of cappers for the percussion rifleman are Tedd Cash's Capper *(left)*, copied from an original which appeared in the classic, "The Muzzleloading Caplock Rifle" by Ned Roberts, and the more commonly seen straightline capper *(right)*, this one made by Uncle Mike's (note how metal loop folds over to hold plunger for easier loading of caps). I keep a leather thong on my capper so I can wear it around my neck while hunting.

as long as you might reasonably expect. The people making these items are usually honest, dedicated craftsmen, but they have an aversion to being rushed. So order your handmade items in the spring if planning for a fall hunt, and be sure to inform the supplier of the exact date you must have his product. If he cannot deliver and you do not wish to wait longer, order from someone else.

Cappers are an important and necessary item for the percussion shooter, for there are few things more frustrating than trying to fit that little bitty No. 10 or No. 11 cap on that teeny tiny nipple when it is 12 degrees below and your fingers have swollen up to the size of salamis, and that magnificent ten-point buck in front of you still has not moved. By far, the straight line capper (so-called because of its straight, brass-tube design) is the most widely used version, but another excellent style, also fashioned after an original, is the Tedd Cash Capper. Tedd has been around a long time and is well-known for the quality parts he makes for muzzleloading rifles. His capper is of the same fine workmanship. It is available in either brass or flashy game-spooking German silver (guess which one I use). Of the quality straight-line cappers on the market, Lyman makes an excellent version that features two steel springs to keep those elusive caps from slipping out prematurely. The Uncle Mike's straight-line capper has a steel lanyard loop that holds back the follower, making it possible to load the capper with only one hand. All three versions work equally well with both foreign and domestic caps (an important but often overlooked consideration). The Cash Capper holds 65 caps and the straight line versions both hold approximately 20, more than you should be able to use or lose in a single day of hunting.

Powder measures are not something to be overly concerned with for the hunter using pre-measured charges, as most of his loads are prepared at home. However, I always throw one in with my gear just out of habit; I have yet to use it on a hunt. Just be sure the measure you select is adjustable to at least 100 grains, in 10-grain increments. A few measures, such as Lyman's, Uncle Mike's, and one sold by Dixie, go to 120 grains; but none go over that amount, a situation of concern only to those hunters going after big game such as bear and elk with a round ball rifle. It just means you'll have to take a little longer in preparing your pre-measured charges.

This hunter-oriented item from The Hawken Shop is a heavy duty black steel cap-per. Although bulkier than more conventional brass cappers, I found this to be an advantage when your hands are numb from the cold, as the capper is easier to grasp, even with gloves on. When ordering, be sure to specify whether it is for Italian or American caps, as they will not work interchangeably, a disadvantage to this item.

Dixie Gun Works' Pan Primer helps ensure ignition for your flintlock.

Two handy items which will help make your one-and-only shot on the hunt a surefire one is a brass nipple primer for percussion guns or a pan primer for flintlocks. Both of these items give added insurance that an adequate, igniting quantity of powder will reach your main charge in the barrel. The nipple primer, which is sold by Dixie Gun Works, is placed over the nipple and jiggled, thereby filling the vent hole and nipple with powder and insuring instantaneous ignition from the cap. The flintlock pan primer spout is simply pressed down into the flashpan; the spring-loaded mechanism thereby releases a goodly amount of FFFFG to prime your lock, with the spout being used to push some extra powder into the touch-hole. This convenient device is also available from Dixie Gun Works and a similar version is made by Uncle Mike's. Either one will help make your rifle speak more reliably on a hunt.

Most muzzleloading hunting rifles and shotguns now come with stainless steel nipples, an improvement over the softer blued steel versions prominent just a few years ago. (If your frontloader does have these softer metal nipples, replace them before your next

Dixie Gun Works' Nipple Primer provides sure-fire insurance for the percussion hunting rifle.

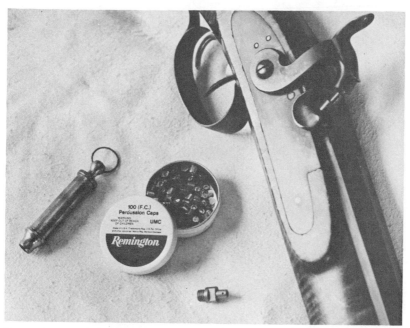

Even a caplock is not foolproof, but these three aces-in-the-hole will help you get your game: nipple charger, Remington Hot Caps, and Uncle Mike's Hot Shot Nipple.

hunt; the stainless versions hold up better and will not corrode as easily.) However, for serious big game hunting, I recommend putting the Uncle Mike's Hot Shot nipple on your frontloader. This unique vented nipple was originally designed to create a hotter flash on percussion guns using Pyrodex, but I have found that the Hot Shot guarantees almost surefire ignition with every percussion gun (except underhammer versions, which are not recommended for use with the Hot Shot). In addition, the use of the Hot Shot nipple will increase your muzzle velocity by about 3 percent, while helping disperse gases that can cause hammer blow-back when firing heavy-duty loads. The only rifle that comes with the Hot Shot as standard equipment is the Trail Guns Armory Kodiak Double Rifle. So unless you have a TGA side-by-side, you can add to the efficiency of your rifle or shotgun by equipping it with this unique nipple; it is an inexpensive and worthwhile improvement.

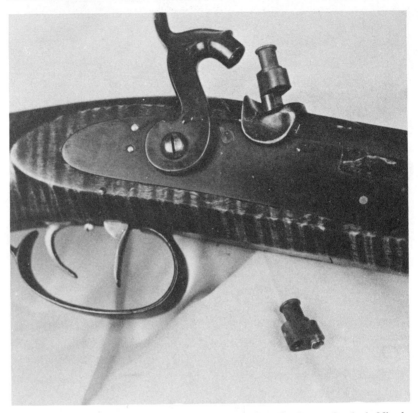

One method for keeping your powder dry: the Butler Creek Caplock Nipple Cover, which I helped conceive.

For flinters, Uncle Mike's has also developed a stainless steel Touch Hole Liner that produces the same *venturi* effect as the Hot Shot nipple. It comes with an Allen wrench and should be installed by a gunsmith who is experienced with black powder arms, although it should fit Dixie's flintlock version of their Tennessee Mountain Rifle and other replaceable touch-hole liners with a ¼ × 28 thread without too much trouble.

It is readily apparent that one of the most important responsibilities a muzzleloading hunter has is to keep his smokepole in a state of readiness during the hunt. At no time is this more critical than during inclement weather. At times I have used everything from plastic baggies to gobs of grease in a sometimes successful effort to keep the "wet look" off of my rifle. Consequently, as one who has been "fortunate" enough to have hunted more than his fair share in rain and snow, I was instrumental in helping to conceive this next item. I can vouch from personal experience that it works. It is the Butler Creek rainproof Nipple Cover for percussion guns. This fingernail-sized plastic device is a tight-fitting cap that covers and thereby waterproofs the nipple, preventing moisture from seeping into the breech and rendering your hunting charge useless. The nipple cover also has a compartment for carrying a spare No. 11 cap. This long-needed item was born in a Rocky Mountain rainstorm a few hunting seasons ago. I had just ridden into camp after coming through a drenching downpour that was topped off by a stimulating horseback ride across an icy river. The waters were so high that my

Another method for keeping your powder dry: the Leather Lock Cover (for both flintlock and percussion rifle) which you can make yourself from scrap, or buy ready-made from Dixie Gun Works. Be sure to waterproof the leather before autumn and keep those tie-downs loose while on the hunt.

saddle scabbard was soaked and I was forced to carry my Hawken over the pommel, with my parka thrown over it and the saddlehorn to keep the rainwater out. Bill Heckerman, President of Butler Creek Corporation, had heard that I was out looking for some winter meat, and he had driven up to our base camp in the inclement weather just to say "Howdy." As I sloshed into the cook's tent, my first words (to nobody in particular, as I recall) were, "Why in the #$%¢ doesn't somebody make a @#$% nipple cover for my #$%¢ Hawken so I can spend more time huntin', and less time trying to keep the @#$! water out?" Well, all good things come to those who cuss a lot, and a few weeks later, Bill sent me a prototype of the new nipple protector. I have used them ever since; they come six to a package, are inexpensive enough so you will not lie awake nights should you lose one, and are small enough to carry wherever you and your rifle go. As an added bonus, if your hunting rifle does not feature a hooked breech or you simply do not wish to break the barrel down for cleaning, the Butler Creek Nipple Cover can be placed over the nipple to seal the breech, so that the barrel can be filled with hot water to flush out the grime.

Speaking of cleaning, there always seem to be a few shooters who take great pleasure in boasting that they don't clean their black powder arms until days, weeks, or even months after a hunt. This

Pipe cleaners are an inexpensive and handy aid for in-the-field maintenance of your muzzleloader.

These two compasses are ideally suited for the muzzleloading hunter; Marble's makes this compact compass *(left)* that takes up very little space in pocket or possibles bag. I keep a leather thong around mine so that I can grasp it easier. On the right this sundial compass, for daytime use only, not only tells you what direction to take, but gives the time of day as well. It is an exact copy of the 1750-era instrument found in the remains of an officer's hut of Rogers Rangers. Available from La Pelleterie and Dixie Gun Works.

is an insult to the art of black powder hunting as well as to muzzleloading guns themselves. When black powder is fired, it leaves a moist, salty residue that immediately begins acting upon the metal of your gun. In time, this causes rust and eventually pitting and corrosion. My guns cost me a lot of hard-earned money and I can't afford to have them become damaged. In his classic book, *The Muzzle Loading Caplock Rifle*, Ned Roberts admonished that the first thing the nineteenth century hunter did upon returning to camp was to clean his rifle. *Then* he cleaned himself, ate, and slept. Even though today's rifles are made with better steels than the originals, black powder hasn't changed all that much — it *still* corrodes! Therefore, if you plan to have your rifle grow old with you, clean it as soon as you get back to camp. Unlike a few years ago, there are numerous

In-the-field cleaners, such as SS1 black powder solvent by Totally Dependable Products, provide quick and effortless temporary protection for muzzleloading firearms.

commercial solvents available today, but the best I've found is still hot, soapy water, followed by dry patches, and a thin coat of oil.

Of course, out in the field, water and a fire to heat it with are not always available. In this case, there are three excellent commercial black powder solvents that cut fouling in a minimum of time and are conveniently packaged in small, unbreakable plastic bottles so that they may easily be transported on any hunt. These solvents, which all work equally well, are Spit-Bath (a pink, bubbly brew manufactured by the Hodgdon Powder Company), Ol' Griz (an ammonia-based blend from The Hawken Shop), and Olde Time Bore Cleaner (a pungent-smelling concoction from CVA). There is also an effective black powder cleaner and solvent called SS1 (packaged in an aerosol can by Totally Dependable Products), but this oil-based spray is extremely penetrating, and care must be taken to keep it from leaking into the nipple or touch-hole areas and dampening your powder for the next day's hunt. But no matter what cleaner you use, always be sure that the nipple and touch-hole are cleaned, dried, and kept free of debris.

After each day's hunt and after cleaning, your muzzleloader should be wiped down with a light coat of oil. Try to stay away from those super-penetrating space-age solutions that can seep into the powder areas, or which will harm the wood of your stock. For general use, I prefer a non-freezing oil, such as that put out by Marble's, or TufOil, a teflon-based solution that is also excellent for smoothing up sticky actions. Totally Dependable Products makes a handy plunger-type container filled with a fine lubricant called SS2, but again, caution should be used when cleaning a charged gun to keep this solution away from the nipple/touch-hole areas. In every case, be sure to wipe the oil from the bore before loading for the hunt; oil-soaked powder may not rust, but it won't ignite either! And unless hunting in extremely wet weather, it is a good practice to wipe the oil from the gun's exterior to keep dust, dirt, and bugs from sticking to the metal during your journey afield.

A good skinning knife is essential for the big game hunter and this Model 104 Twinset by Buck is one of the best, featuring a skinning and capping blade which also doubles for small game.

When venturing far from civilization on a hunt, one of my biggest fears is the thought of breaking a ramrod. After all, a muzzle-loading hunter without a ramrod is through for the day, unless of course, he happens to have very long, strong and thin fingers! For years I used to carry an old .50 caliber U.S. Army cleaning rod, which unscrews in four sections, which makes it easy to pack in a shooting bag or coat pocket. When reloading, I often used the front section with the handle as a short starter, then I screwed all the pieces together and rammed the ball home. However, it has come to my attention that this hard metal rod, used over a period of years, can cause excessive muzzle wear to your rifle, eventually decreasing its accuracy. The same danger exists with the new fiberglass ram-rods, although this can be alleviated to an extent by using the brass Muzzle Guard manufactured by Uncle Mike's. In an effort to find a solution to the breaking problem of wooden ramrods that normally come with our hunting rifles, I discovered that many of the old-timers used to soak their ramrods in kerosene until the wood was completely saturated. This did not make the rod totally unbreakable, but it did give it a greater resiliency. However, there are two new portable ramrods that can give worry-wart hunters like myself renewed confidence in the field.

The first of these is the superb three-piece stainless steel ramrod sold by Uncle Mike's. This device assembles into a 30-inch length to reach to the breech end of most barrels and fits all popular calibers. However, Kentucky rifle shooters will have to purchase the extra extension Uncle Mike's makes to traverse the entire barrel of their long guns. The three-piece rod features a wooden ball handle on one end and a threaded tip on the other for screwing in various attachments, such as a cleaning jag.

The second device is even more unique, as it was not originally designed for black powder hunting, but it works when used within its limitations. It is called the Flex-Gun Rod, and consists of a flexible length of coiled metallic cable with a screw-in attachment adaptor on one end and a patch-holding swivel-loop on the other. The Flex-Rod easily coils up to fit into the 4-inch plastic pouch that comes with it. When uncoiled, the cable becomes a ridged rod with enough stiffness to ram home a loose-fitting ball or greased Mini. The rod was the invention of Victor Malesky, a Michigan hunter who originally devised the Flex-Rod to remove barrel obstructions from rifles and shotguns in the field. He gave prototypes of the rod to each of his grandsons so that they would never be bothered by this potentially dangerous problem. It is one of these grandsons, Larry Malesky, who now heads up the Flex-Gun Rod Company. When I first met Larry, he was marketing his product strictly as a cleaning aid for (pardon the expression) cartridge arms, but it caught my eye as a great emergency device for the muzzleloading hunter. It helps to use the rod first to wipe the bore in order to clean out fouling from your previous shot, thereby making reloading easier. Be sure to try a few practice sessions on the shooting range beforehand and mark the Flex-Rod with masking tape so that you will know that the ball is firmly seated on your powder charge before you fire. The Flex-Rod is not as sturdy as a regular ramrod, but in an emergency, it does the job as long as the bore is not heavily fouled and the projectile slides down easily. The Flex-Rod comes in 36-inch lengths (Model CRS) or a more versatile 46-inch (Model BPR) which I

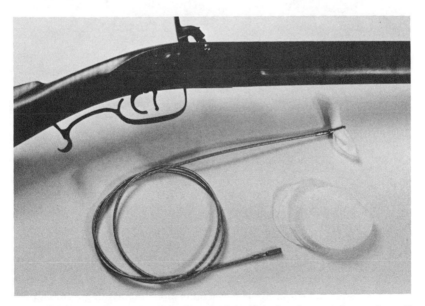

Special BPR Model of the Flex-Gun Rod is 46 inches long and can clean all muzzleloading rifles. It also can serve as an emergency ramrod if all proper safety precautions are followed.

Everyone, man and beast, needs a cool drink along the hunting trail, and this handmade, authentic blackpowder-era canteen is truly refreshing. The inside is waterproofed with melted wax, just as the originals were. It's available from Dixie Gun Works.

originally suggested to Larry as an addition to his line. You may
wish to have a brass ramrod tip threaded to fit the shotgun brush
adaptor, although the extra tips I have seem to work fine. Oh yes,
you can also use the Flex-Rod to clean your rifle, the purpose for
which it was originally intended.

Other products which I have found to be of help in my hunting
activities are depicted throughout the rest of this chapter. However,
one unique item which is not shown (mainly because it photographs
about as well as a close-up of a bowl of split-pea soup) is something
that no cold-weather hunter should be without: the various brands
of chemical heat packets, which sell under a variety of names. On
one winter hunt under blizzard conditions (not something I planned,
but it did provide a "natural" opportunity to do some product testing), I took along ten heat pads marketed under the brand Hot Mini
24, the theory being that the pad will stay hot for twenty-four hours.
The idea behind these novel little items is that when a seal is pulled
away from the pad, thereby letting air mix with the chemicals within the 4-by-6-inch packet, it starts to generate heat within fifteen
minutes. From actual use, I can testify that this happens, although
not for the twenty-four hour span advertised, at least, not in the
higher 10,000-foot elevations in which I was hunting. I suspect that
the heat may last longer in lower elevations for desert hunting or on
the Great Plains. Still, the Hot Mini did throw out a lot of welcomed
heat for a full five hours, enough time to permit me to still hunt
longer than I normally would have. The Hot Mini was also a great
companion to take into my bedroll at night, zipping up the goose
down around me and placing that little sucker on my chest. If my
wife ever leaves me, I'm moving in with a Hot Mini. Get some and
try them on your next bad-weather hunt. I suspect duck hunters will
fall in love with them, too. But artificial warmers aside, there is still
no substitute for being properly clothed, an important (and perhaps
surprising) topic we will take up in the next chapter.

CHAPTER SEVEN

THE HUNTER'S CLOTHING

J ust because you're hunting with a nineteenth century-style rifle doesn't mean you have to dress like a nineteenth-century pioneer — not that there's anything wrong with that. I enjoy seeing a properly outfitted buckskin 'n' beaded mountain man or homespun Colonial touching off his long gun on the target range or at rendezvous. But out in today's forest and field, it's a different story. Years ago the frontiersman's life depended upon his ability to blend in with his natural surroundings. Today, in most cases, a hunter's life depends upon his *not* blending in with his surroundings. I hate to say it, but the woods still harbor a small population of mental slobs (I refuse to call them "hunters" for they do not deserve that dignity) who will take a snap shot at your elkskin hunting coat and apologize later, that is, if there is anything left to apologize to.

The unfortunate fact is, that to the untrained eye, buckskins tend to make you look like whatever happens to be in season. Therefore, the First Commandment of Muzzleloading Clothing is to save those 'skins for more formal occasions. Don't get me wrong; I own a fringed pair of hunting pants plus a tailored "St. Louis suit" of buckskins, but I only wear them on specific non-hunting situations, such as on Kit Carson's birthday and my wedding anniversary — never on a hunt. The only two exceptions to this rule are: 1) when hunting color-conscious game, such as turkey or ducks (even then, "still" hunting is the norm and the camouflaged hunter restricts not only his visibility, but movement as well. More about this in Chapter Eight); 2) when you are hunting on a private preserve, and know there are no other nimrods around who might accidentally ventilate your sinew with a patched round ball (or worse yet!) with a mis-aimed jacketed hollow point.

Buckskins may be picturesque, but they can make you look too much like a deer to other hunters. Save those 'skins for rendezvous.

Besides the safety factor, there are practical reasons for leaving your buckskins back at the lodge. They are clammy-cold in the winter, and sweaty-hot in the summer. They also tend to hold water when wet and will occasionally shrink in the most awkward places. They do look good, however, and around the campfire, after the day's hunt, they lend a flavor of long ago. But keep them separate from the hunt. After all, they sure did not help the deer that had them before you.

What then, should the muzzleloading hunter of today wear? Basically the same clothing as any twentieth century hunter, although a few practical concessions can be made. For most black powder hunters, the most conspicuous item of wearing apparel is the hat. I realize that not everyone wears a hat when hunting, but I have found it to be as practical as it is picturesque. Our forefathers knew what they were doing when they donned their wide-brimmed felt headgear. The 3- to 4-inch brim is the best means I've found for keeping rain and snow off of your face, which is especially useful if, like me, you wear glasses. And of course, the wide-brimmed hat has long been known for keeping the sun out of one's eyes; a bit of shade is welcomed on warm days, and it helps prevent sunburn, particularly when desert hunting or in high altitudes, where ultraviolet rays can be severely harsh.

Although you may find numerous shapes and styles of "buckskinner's hats" advertised in the various muzzleloading magazines, do not let price override quality. A good hat is not cheap, but an inexpensive one will literally shred apart during the first rainstorm. Felt hat quality is generally measured by "X's"; the more "X's" stamped inside a hat's liner or sweatband, the better the quality of felt. For hunting, I have found anything with four "X's" (XXXX) or better will serve you long and wear well. As an added bonus, after you have been lucky enough to get caught in two or three downpours, the brim will assume a graceful dip fore and aft, giving you a truly authentic "muzzleloader's look." Of course, you can speed things up a bit by shaping the brim and crown to any configuration you want by holding it over a jet of steam from the kitchen teapot and molding the felt with your hands.

Basically, there are three distinct hat styles for the muzzleloading hunter to choose. The first is the wide-brim, rounded-crown

Mormon Hat, as depicted in the accompanying photograph. This is the hat I most often wear on my hunts, and it has even less shape now than is shown, a situation brought about by my using it to carry water and fan fires (not necessarily at the same time). My particular Mormon Hat is made by Eddy Brothers, is a five-X quality beaver fur, and comes in brown, black, and gray. I bought mine years ago at The Buffalo Robe, but other buckskinner's clothing stores also carry this brand.

Having seen first hand how well a five-X hat can take a beating lo these many years, I was duly intrigued when a firm known as C&H Traders came out with two authentic styles of mountain man *ten-X* beaver fur felt hats, the Taos Trapper's Hat (appearing somewhat like the Mormon Hat, but with a lower, earlier-styled rounded crown) and the Rocky Mountain Hat, with a 4-inch-wide brim and a 4-inch high flat crown. I could not let apparent quality such as this go unnoticed, so I promptly ordered the Rocky Mountain Hat and was definitely not disappointed. Equally impressive was the C&H Traders guarantee that comes with each hat: "Please let us know if there is something wrong with your hat, we will be glad to make it right." There is nothing wrong with their hat, except that when you take it out of its storage box, it seems almost too pretty to use for hunting. But then I felt the same way about my Eddy Brothers hat when I first got it. A few deer seasons will put it right! Either style of C&H hat is available in black, brown, or tan (which really appears gray to my eye). Unlike the other hats listed in this chapter which can be purchased ready-made, the C&H product is fashioned one at a time, per your order, so be sure to allow about two months for delivery. This firm also makes a lower priced "wool felt hat," but for the serious hunter who wants a hat he can rely on in all kinds of weather, order only the C&H beaver fur; you won't be disappointed.

Another maker of excellent hats for the hunter is the well-known firm of Stetson. A wide spectrum of colors for both men and women plus a variety of crown shapes and heights and brim widths is available, although you may have to go to a number of western wear stores to see the complete array. I own three Stetsons that I have purchased over the years, but my favorite is a 3-inch brim "Renegade" that is four-X quality; I use this hat almost exclusively

Be prepared for anything, no matter what the weather may bring. Riding out for a day's hunt, I am wearing a wide brimmed hat, goose down vest, and cotton shirt. Jacket and rain poncho are tied to the saddle.

for one-day hunts, such as small game hunting and shotgunning. I like it so much, I also wear it around town, where it has become something of a trademark. My wife claims that my Stetson makes me easier to spot in a crowd, but I suspect any of the hats listed here will do that. Because the Stetson is of such high quality, I have never understood why they chose to detract from their product by encircling the crown of some of their styles with a plastic hatband. Two of my Stetsons had this malady and I promptly replaced the plastic with more appropriate bands; my black dress hat now sports a horsehair band and the "Renegade" has a plain leather band with my initials, fashioned for me by famed Hollywood saddlemaker Ed Bohlin. Both my Eddy Brothers and C&H mountain man hats retain the ribbon bands they originally came with. For those of you who want to add a little more authentic color to your headgear, beaded bands may be obtained from C&H Traders as well as from some of the muzzleloading supply houses and clothiers listed in Chapter Ten.

As versatile as the wide-brimmed hat may be, cold weather hunting often dictates another, equally authentic style of hat for the muzzleloader, the fur cap. Original styles, dating from the 1800's through the 1870's, were often fashioned from the tanned, fur-covered hides of bear, beaver, fox, wolf, and raccoon. Sometimes these hats were lined with wool or felt and sported a narrow leather visor-like brim. Many individual craftsmen are reproducing these hats and they are just as effective today as they were 150 years ago. However, because they are not a mass-produced item, they may be difficult to locate. Your best bet is to check the classified ads in the various muzzleloading magazines and contact some of the buck-skinners' clothing shops listed in Chapter Ten. If you are willing to make a minor allowance in authenticity, there is, however, a ready-made fur hat that is quite a bargain for the money. It is the French rabbit-fur Trooper's Hat sold by the respected firm of L.L. Bean. Although styled more like the 1940's rather than the 1840's, this extremely well-made hat is "of the spirit," as you can see from the photos of me and my elk in Chapter Two. The inside of the hat is quilt-lined and features wool ear flaps that fold down. Of course, the fur-covered side flaps and front visor also fold down to shield the cheeks and forehead during extreme cold. If you cannot find an-

A heavy coat and fur cap was just as highly regarded for cold weather hunting in the nineteenth century as it is now, even if our forefathers did not know what "chill factor" meant.

other fur style you like, this hat combines quality and price to make an ideal cold weather companion. Even when wearing my wide-brimmed hat on late autumn or early spring hunts, I always pack the Bean hat along. Of course, there is nothing wrong with the traditional coonskin caps, such as sold by Dixie, as long as you don't mind a tail wagging down the back of your neck.

Other styles of hunter's caps from the black powder era seem to be more decorative than useful. Nonetheless, they are picturesque and authentic and should be discussed since they do not detract from the hunter's effectiveness. Dixie Gun Works sells a homespun, hand-knitted wool Liberty Cap, the type of nightcap-styled, tasseled headgear worn by American troops of the Revolutionary War and French traders of the mountain man era. La Pelleterie makes an 1830's era Hunter's Hood from Hudson Bay blankets; this wool hood drapes over the head and can be decorated with beads and feathers. This same firm also makes a Canadian Cap, which appears somewhat like a wool beanie with fur trim. Ben Franklin wore one, but not to hunt; he took his to Paris.

Another useful item for every hunter is the bandana, a simple, large square piece of cloth that can be stuffed in the back pocket and used to wipe the sweat from your brow, the dirt from your hands, the grunge from your rifle, and when placed over your nose and mouth "outlaw" style, even keeps blowing dust out of your lungs. Dampened with water from your canteen and tied around your neck, it adds a refreshing touch to help ease discomfort while hunting during the hotter part of the day.

The shirts I normally wear while hunting vary from light cotton to heavy 10-ounce chamois, depending on where I am hunting and the time of year. As most hunting is done during the fall, when the icy chill of early morning can turn into the stifling heat of afternoon, multiple layers of clothing are quite effective, so that outer garments may be removed (or added) as the temperature changes. I prefer wearing a cotton T-shirt, then a medium-weight flannel shirt, followed by a goose down vest, and finally a coat. On my Rocky Mountain bear and elk hunts, I also wear longjohns, which in addition to keeping goosebumps away, also keep your knees from rubbing raw if you are on horseback for any length of time. Rather than climb into the colorful red one-piece "Union Suit," I opt for a set of flannel longjohn bottoms, with a separate "River Driver's" longjohn top; each of which can be easily stripped off if it gets too warm during the day. Both of these items can be ordered from L.L. Bean or Eddie Bauer if your local sporting goods store does not carry them. Wool pants and shirts are also durable and functional items if the hunter can wear them without itching and scratching himself into oblivion. I cannot, a situation especially disastrous when still hunting. Hence, my preference for cotton and flannel.

I began hearing so much about "fishnet undershirts," a close-fitting, crossknit form of T-shirt, that I finally bought some to take on a hunting trip along the foggy coast of Northern California. The theory is that this open-air shirt keeps you warmer in the winter and cooler in the summer, somewhat like a heat pump. However, after my three-day hunt, I was not convinced that this shirt kept me any warmer or cooler than my traditional cotton T-shirt, but it did place a black and blue cross-hatch mark on my shoulder when I finally took a boar with my .54 caliber Hawken. I ended up giving the shirts to my wife, who looks much better in them than I do.

For pants, any heavy-duty, non-rustling variety of denim, flannel or khaki will do (not corduroy, as it sometimes makes a "swishing" sound when you walk, which could alert game; why take the chance?). The more pockets your pants have, the better off you are. Bush pants are ideal for hunting, as patches, caps, flints, and all manner of accessories can be conveniently stored in the two roomy pockets on each leg; these pants are sold by most outdoors outfitters such as Norm Thompson, Bean, and Bauer.

One of the most useful items for the black powder hunter of to-day is the bush coat. This one single item can effectively carry all the shooting equipment a flintlock or percussion hunter will need, and still have room left over for a sandwich or two. (In cold weather, a heavy shirt and/or a down vest is worn under the bush coat.) The bush coat is especially useful to those hunters who do not wish to become a victim of their own possibles bag, as described in the preceding chapter.

Most bush coats come with four expandable pockets, two on each side. By placing specific items in each pocket, with a little practice you will soon find yourself unconsciously finding the desired item with a minimum of time-consuming search; there is no game-spooking mumbling and fumbling as sometimes results from frantically searching through a possibles bag, an exercise that often reminds me of a woman going through her purse looking for a lipstick (no sexist remarks intended, but that *is* how it looks). When hunting with a percussion rifle, I keep my pre-measured charges in the lower right-hand pocket; the left-hand pocket is reserved for the

Here's proof that you don't have to wear buckskins in order to take game in buckskinner fashion. Toby Bridges dropped this hefty boar with a custom muzzleloader from Dixie Gun Works.

empty tubes. In this way, I can keep track of how many shots I've fired and how many I have remaining. Thus, it becomes an easy exercise in speed loading to hold the rifle, butt on the ground, muzzle up, with my left hand, and with my right hand pluck a charged Quick Loader from my right pocket, flip open the cap with my thumb, pour powder down the bore, reverse the Quick Loader to drop in the pre-greased Mini (patched balls will take slightly longer), withdraw the ramrod with that same right hand and ram the charge home. The ramrod is replaced (or if it is a quick second shot, I jam it into the ground or more often simply hold it next to the rifle forestock with my left hand), then just cap and shoot. My upper left pocket carries a "trouble kit," a small buckskin bag containing a nipple wrench, small screwdriver, extra nipple, and a nipple pick. (The capper, an elusive item at best, is hung around my neck via a leather thong. Be sure to tuck the capper into your shirt to keep it from rattling.) When carrying a flintlock, the only additional items I add are extra flints wrapped in a small piece of leather to keep them from slicing up my fingers, and a brass pan charger, which is kept in my lower right-hand pocket along with my pre-measured charges. On those not-too-frequent occasions when I use a patched round ball (primarily for small game), I keep an extra supply of Teflon-coated Ox-Yoke patches in my upper right-hand pocket to quickly replace one that may drop off of the muzzle while loading. Of course, these same patches are also packed in with a ball in my Quick Loader. I also carry a cut-down Short Starter but rarely use it due to the time it takes; a slightly undersized ball and a pre-greased, pre-cut patch can easily be seated for a second shot using just your ramrod.

Thus, you have everything you need for reloading, conveniently accessible and well-balanced on your body. Of course, I always carry a knife on my belt and matches in my pants pocket, but we will get into that in Chapter Eight. See how everything ties together?

Footwear can literally be a sore point if you insist on following in your forefather's moccasin prints. Even with thick leather soles, moccasins will let you feel every pebble, rock and twig under or alongside your feet. They may muffle your footsteps, but the silence will be broken by your screams of pain. However, mocs are fine for around the campfire; I always take along a pair for after-the-hunt relaxation, when I can let my boots walk themselves over to a corner to air out. Surprisingly, there are a great variety of handmade moccasins available from dedicated outfitters who specialize in frontier clothing. One of the most versatile styles is called The Prairie Boot, and features a wrap-around buckskin top and a non-slip composition sole. I have a pair and often wear them around the house as well as in camp—they are that comfortable. I also have a pair of beaded deerskin moccasins with a thick leather sole stitched on the bottom for added protection. It is basically a plains-type moccasin. These two styles, plus a few more, are available from The Buffalo Robe and La Pelleterie. They are all individually hand-cut and sewn from a pattern of your foot, which you must trace on a piece of (preferably brown for authenticity) wrapping paper, which gives you an idea of the custom fit you will receive.

Although Carson and Colter may have worn moccasins, men like Fremont and Ruxton did not. From practical experience, I choose to follow their lead and always wear thick-soled leather footwear. Leather helps repel snakebites, rocks, and rainwater. That is why, for the hunting trail, there is nothing like good-fitting, well-made boots. They are a necessity. When hunting on horseback, hiking boots can also be worn, as long as the toe will fit into your stirrup comfortably and you can kick free in a hurry if you have to. However, I wear riding boots fitted with a walking heel, as the horses are usually tied up a good half-mile from where our actual hunting will be taking place. Boots can be either the lace-up or pull-on variety, as long as they cover over the ankle to lend support. Mail order firms such as Browning, Gokeys, Bean, and Gander Mountain make excellent boots if you cannot find a suitable pair from a shoe store or sporting goods dealer near you. Beware of some synthetic materials that will not permit your feet to "breathe", thereby creating an unhealthy sweaty-foot situation. Although it is slightly more expensive, I still have found real leather to be the best buy for practical use. Be sure to get your boots at least two months before the hunt, and take some evening walks with them over the hunting socks you plan to wear. That way they will be broken in by the time you really need them; should your boots turn out to be uncomfortable or cause blisters, you will have time to exchange them (and your blisters will have time to heal) before your hunt. Nothing breaks a hunter's concentration more quickly than sore feet, unless, of course, he is also cold and wet.

I have found a goose down vest is one of the best means of insuring my comfort from cold. Worn with a shirt or under a coat, it provides an extra margin of warmth, yet when not needed, can be tightly rolled up and stuffed into a day pack or tied onto the back of your belt. It also makes a handy pillow for those mid-afternoon siestas, when nothing is stirring but the flies.

Around the campfire or homefire, mocassins provide welcome relief from boots after the day's hunt. These beaded mocs are from The Buffalo Robe.

The muzzleloading hunter of the twentieth century can be more efficient without buckskins. Hunter's orange vest is worn over bush coat, which affords more pockets than a possibles bag for shooting implements.

There are also vests and coats made of duck down (less expensive than goose down but not as good an insulator) and even synthetic materials, such as Hollofil and PolarGuard. These synthetics will not matt up and lose their insulating properties (like the real stuff does) when wet, but they also do not compress as tightly for packing and they are slightly heavier. However, they do permit your body to "breathe" while keeping in natural heat, just as goose down does. The final selection is up to you. For added versatility, some vests come with a reversible camouflage print on one side and day-glo orange on the other.

If there is one color that every muzzleloading hunter should wear, it is International (or Hunter's) Orange, by far the most visible color in the spectrum. Some states, such as Wyoming, require that it be worn while in the field during any open season. It is a good rule and makes common sense, although there is a belief that some animals, even though colorblind, can spot the orange color if there is movement. But if you are moving, chances are that you will be detected anyway. Whether or not animals can see you when you are wearing orange, other hunters most certainly will, and that's what hunter safety is all about. The easiest method of literally playing it safe is to wear one of those inexpensive plastic vests found in most gun stores. Just slip it over your outer garment, unless, of course, your outer garment is already an orange color. Although commonly practiced by some hunters, I personally do not like the idea of wrapping orange tape around my muzzleloading rifle, as it destroys the esthetic look of the gun and can damage the finish on the stock. However, I did come across a novel way for black powder shooters to show their color, so to speak, which I will pass on to you (like most good ideas, this one was not mine, either). I was hunting with an outfitter a few autumns ago when one of the wranglers came riding in with an orange knit watch cap stretched over the crown of his Stetson. He had cut off the top of the knit cap (not the Stetson!) so that it could be pulled down over the top of the crown, like a giant orange hat band. Seemed like a good idea, so I thought I would pass it on. That wrangler probably has his own spread by now.

As with all forms of hunting, black powder or otherwise, it pays to be prepared for all kinds of weather. That means taking a warm coat, preferably one which will not fall apart. I mention this because one September, while rushing to leave the house in order to be at my appointed spot on opening day of deer season, I hurriedly grabbed an old hunting coat that I had worn for years, and frantically put it on. My wife watched with interest as the sleeve ripped right off the coat and fell to the floor. There I was, wearing a one-armed vest! The lesson: Be sure to pre-check your hunting clothes just as thoroughly as you pre-check your hunting muzzleloader. I always do . . . now.

While we are on the subject of cold-weather clothing, there is a stylish item that has retained its versatility for almost 200 years. It is the capote, a heavy winter coat made from Hudson's Bay blankets and used by French explorers in the Northeast during the 1700's, officers and men in the Revolutionary Army, as well as trap-

Still-hunting keen-eyed birds such as ducks, geese, and turkeys is one of the rare occasions when visibility must be sacrificed to achieve hunting success.

This superb and comfortable camouflage suit helped me bag a Spring gobbler in Texas. The two-piece flannel outfit is made by Melton Shirt Company and marketed through many well-known outfitters, such as L. L. Bean.

Hudson's Bay Capote or Duffle Coat is a 200-year-old style of garment that provides surprising warmth. This Duffle Coat was made by La Pelleterie.

pers and traders of the early nineteenth century in the Far West. Capotes were also worn by the Plains Indians, most notably the Crow, Sioux, and Blackfeet. This heavy winter coat comes in the varied colors and stripes of the Hudson Bay blanket, features a wind-breaking hood, and can be lined or unlined, fringed, beaded, or plain. It is a warm, serviceable and good-looking item that is as useful to the black powder hunter of today as it was to his great-great-grandfather. Excellent capotes are handcrafted by La Pelleterie and The Buffalo Robe. These two firms also make trapper's mittens and matching gun covers fashioned from the same heavy wool Hudson's Bay blankets as your capote.

Some hunters give their muzzleloaders better treatment than they give themselves. This is especially true in wet weather hunting. I have seen more than one still-hunter hunched over his smokepole, in a drizzle, effectively shielding the precious lock area with his rain-soaked body. By all means carry a poncho, rolled up and tied to your belt, stuffed in a day pack, or even crammed in your coat pocket. Ponchos are far more effective for the muzzleloading hunter than raincoats, for they can be used to cover the entire gun, as well as yourself. They are available in orange, yellow, or camouflage from most of the outdoor suppliers.

It may appear that there are more modern outdoors clothes than "old-timey" ones in a book devoted to preserving the art of black powder hunting. The simple fact is that, in order to be effective (i.e., to enjoy yourself whether or not you down game), the muzzleloading hunter must be as comfortable as possible. The spirit of romance is in the mind, not on the body. Yet, where certain articles of early American clothing prove superior, they are retained in the life of the twentieth century hunter.

It is readily apparent that the muzzleloading hunter's clothing is, like himself, a unique combination of old and new. I am opposed to neither, and as new products are produced, or old ones re-discovered, there is a spirit of adventure in testing them on a hunt. However, one item that has no place on any hunter's wearing apparel is the modern-day Velcro fastener, which may be fine for most outdoor sporting clothes, but definitely not for anything a knowledgeable hunter would wear in the field. It produces one of the most unnatural sounds ever to be carried by a mountain breeze. I once

For rainy weather, the poncho is better than a raincoat for the muzzleloader, as it allows him to keep his rifle under the protective cover of the widely cut material, yet it permits freedom of movement for offhand shooting.

spent a bone-chilling four hours, wearing a camouflaged poncho and crouched down behind heavy brush alongside a Rocky Mountain lake, waiting for a black bear to show himself. My hunting partner and I knew he was nearby, for we had seen his sign. It was a dismal late afternoon. A cold mountain fog had settled in around us, an icy mist that crystallized on my eyebrows and beard and made it impossible to feel the heavy .54 Hawken on my lap. My legs were cramped and my muscles screamed for me to stand up and stretch, but still we remained motionless, a shadowy part of the landscape. And then we saw the bruin — a dark distant movement cautiously lumbering within range of my loaded and capped .54. As he was lumbering into range and I was about to cock the hammer of my rifle, my hunting partner "quietly" ripped open his Velcro-fastened coat to get his binoculars. That horrendous sound caused the bear to vanish faster than Houdini could have wished. As long as the silence had been broken, I took advantage of the opportunity to verbally reflect upon my partner's ancestry, with particular focus on his parentage. Of course, I guess there is a good side to the story, as I did not have to clean my rifle that night. To keep his sanity, a hunter should always look for the positive side to everything!

Needless to say, pockets of hunting coats should be flapped to keep from losing their contents, but buttons or tie-downs are best. Snaps and zippers are marginal and nothing else should ever be considered.

Of course, after the hunt, you and your clothes will probably smell like something not of this earth. One of the most embarrassing plane rides I ever had was after a week-long deer hunt in the Sierra Nevadas of Northern California. Due to a successful hunt and the inevitable "celebration" the night after, I was a tad late in catching my plane back to civilization. I barely made it from camp to airport, without a chance to rent a motel room so that I could shave and shower before the trip home, although I did clean and oil my rifle (remember what I said about hunters taking better care of their muzzleloaders?). I checked my caplock and baggage and stumbled into a seat. It was a crowded flight, yet I could not understand why no one was sitting next to me. I even had a difficult time getting the stewardess's attention for lunch. She kept on adjusting the air vents, as did others seated in front and behind me. Of course, having lived with myself and all the other animals of the forest for a full week, I was totally impervious to the reality of the situation. It was only after greeting my wife at home did the true facts become known. She was very diplomatic about it. Never said a word. She just simply took every item of clothing I packed back from that trip, including my socks, and sent them to the dry cleaners!

Photo courtesy of Butler Creek

CHAPTER EIGHT

A CACHE OF LORE
FOR HUNTING SUCCESS

I once asked famed Jackson Hole, Wyoming outfitter Paul Crittenden what he found to be the biggest problem in his profession.

"It's the attitude of some hunters," he replied. "They come into camp thinking, 'It's going to be so simple,' and that they will bag a trophy the first day out. It just isn't that way, no matter how good a hunter a fellow may be."

I will be the first to attest to that. As an example, for years I have heard that bear hunting was easy and that every spring they fall out of the trees like ripe acorns. Well, I would like to set the record straight by stating that I have been black bear hunting for three years in a row without ever seeing a single member of the *Ursus americanus* species. I've seen plenty of tracks, lots of diggings, but no bear. Conversely, I have always been told how difficult elk hunting was. I have personally been assailed by hunters who have spent more than a decade elk hunting, without ever firing a shot. "Don't even bother takin' your rifle on an elk hunt," one dejected fellow advised, "'cause you'll never get a chance to use it." Yet, on my first day elk hunting, I did not shoot a spike elk because I felt he was too small, and later that same day held my fire at a bull because he was out of range of my .54 Sharps. My guide was awestruck. "My Gawd, you've passed up more elk today than most hunters see in a lifetime," he exclaimed incredulously. The next morning at precisely 7:30 a.m. on the first day of autumn, I dropped a six-point bull with a single shot from the big octagon-barreled gun.

After more than a quarter of a century of hunting, I have concluded that a sportsman's success is determined by an equal mix of skill and luck. Unless you know how to shoot and how to hunt, the odds are against you bringing anything home besides sore feet. Yet, even the most skilled outdoorsman is helpless if the weather turns bad or the game, for one reason or the other, has left the area. If there are any keys to hunter success, they are perseverance and organization.

Another phrase for perseverance is positive thinking. It is an essential ingredient for the black powder sportsman. Assuming you have mastered all of the muzzleloading hunter's basic skills, there should not be the slightest doubt that you will ultimately harvest

On the trail of the elusive black bear.

whatever game you set out after. For example, I am convinced that I will eventually get my bear; the law of averages is on my side. Maybe not this year or perhaps the next. But some day, some season, somewhere, I will be successful. On the other hand, the Spirit of the Hunt may be with you on opening day and you will take your trophy the first day out. The main thing is to be prepared, both mentally and physically, and enjoy the hunt, whether you fire a shot or not. Just being alone in the wilderness can be reward enough. Because of this attitude, I once bagged a buck in the hottest part of an August afternoon (when most people will tell you not to hunt). It was California's early deer season and temperatures were up in the 90's. Yet after hunting all morning, I still did not feel like going back to camp. I was sick of the city; this was only a three-day hunt and I wanted to immerse myself in as much of the outdoors as possible in what little time I had. So I began wandering the dry, brushy hills with my heavy caplock rifle cradled in my arm. According to all the rules of common sense and wildlife habits, that buck should have been dozing under the shady crest of a hill, but he wasn't. Somehow our paths crossed. I don't know who was more surprised, but I shouldered my Hawken, fired, and watched that blacktail tumble down a hill to a dirt road below. Luck? Skill? Perseverance? Readiness? A little of each, I think.

As we have already discussed in the preceding chapters, being prepared for a muzzleloading hunt involves a lot of pre-planning. Although I have a special "hunting box" into which I throw everything I feel I might possibly need for my annual autumn excursion, I am always in fear that I will somehow forget that one important item, whatever it may be. Therefore, I have prepared a master list, which I also keep in the hunting box. It serves as a checklist each season and saves me the trouble and pain of rethinking everything. Besides, because of the way my lifestyle is structured, some of my hunts have been last-minute adventures (through no fault of my own, I hasten to add), and there is not always time to scurry around the house, frantically assembling every black powder item I can lay my hands on. Therefore, in the interest of saving you both time and trouble come next Fall, I am herewith duplicating my master list, to which I have added a few more items to make it more applicable to all muzzleloading hunters:

Handy Hacker Checklist for Muzzleloading Hunters

Hunting license and game tag (it's a crime to forget these!)
Rifle
Back-up pistol, belt, and holster
Black powder/Pyrodex (make sure you have the correct granule designation)
Pre-measured tubes
Bullets
Possibles bag (if needed)
Emergency kit for your muzzleloader (screwdriver, nipple wrench and pick, extra nipple, etc.)
Shortstarter
Game bag or cheesecloth for wrapping meat
Orange hunting vest
Capper (for percussion guns)
Bullet/patch lube
Caps or flints (be sure to pack extras)
Cleaning equipment (solvent, rod, patches, cotton swabs, extra rags, oil)
Hunting knife
Sharpening stone
Eating utensils
Cooking pots, pans (if needed)
Canteen
Matches
Flashlight (be sure to check batteries before leaving town)
Bedroll
Tent
Raingear (poncho)
Toilet articles (soap, towel, comb, toothbrush and paste)
Camp moccasins
Hat
Heavy coat
Insulated vest
Underwear, socks (always take along more than you think you'll need)
Longjohns

Extra pair of pants and shirt (in case you get wet)
Reading material
Extra pair of prescription glasses
Medication (allergies, cold pills, vitamins, etc.)
Foot powder
Toilet tissue (most often forgotten and most severely missed!)
Bandana
Camera and film
Rope
Alarm clock (unless your wake-up discipline is better than
    mine)
Compass
Map of area in which you are hunting
Candles (for starting fires with wet wood)
Ax
First aid kit (bandages, gauze, iodine, tape and tweezers)
Bug repellent
Snake bite kit

I have purposely omitted shaving gear (does *anybody* shave while hunting?) and foodstuffs, the latter being a matter of individual tastes and length of the hunt. I usually try to make my meals as easy to prepare as possible, taking dehydrated foods for breakfast (i.e. instant orange drink, tea bags, energy bars) so that I may get out of my bedroll and start hunting as quickly as possible. Lunch consists of things that I can carry with me, such as fruit, energy bars, and sandwiches made the night before. Supper is a time for relaxing after the day's activities and this is usually my biggest meal. (I know that is not what the nutritionists say, but I don't care.) For this main meal I will fix anything from dehydrated full course dinners to canned meats or stews (cooking them right in the opened can, so that there are no pots or pans to wash afterwards). Of course, this is for just the very basic under-the-stars camps. The type of food you take should increase along with the comfort of your facilities (tent, camper, van, cabin, etc.).

On any black powder hunt, whether near or far from home, be sure to carry enough powder and ball. Very few small town stores are equipped to meet the exacting needs of the muzzleloading hunter. I will never forget the story of a good friend of mine who

All downed big game animals should be approached with caution, and if possible from behind.

went on a black powder buffalo hunt armed with an extremely fine custom-made plains rifle, but he took only a half-pound of powder and three bullets. It was to be the hunt of a lifetime but, needless to say, he was sorely disappointed. His first two shots missed and his third only wounded a bull, but did not drop him. The final shot had to be fired by another hunter. Always carry at least ten bullets and pre-measured powder charges on any big game black powder hunt, and twenty charges when going after small, fast-moving game such as squirrel or rabbit.

Although I consider black powder hunting to be a very private, personal experience, I always feel better when I hunt with a partner (preferably also armed with a muzzleloader). The reasons for this are twofold: first, you know you've got a buddy to back you up should your first shot only wound your animal, thereby giving you time to reload. Secondly, should your shot go astray or your rifle misfire, your partner can at least have a shot and perhaps the game will not be lost. Besides making your hunting more productive, a back-up man can also make it safer. Remember, *any* wounded or cornered animal can turn and attack. These aggressive tendencies should not be attributed only to confirmed mankillers. Once while shotgunning alone for doves in a dry wash outside of Tucson, I was repeatedly attacked by a single bird, swooping in at me again and again, aiming for my face. At one point, my Stetson was actually knocked from my head. She was evidently intent upon guarding her nest. Rather than perpetuate this uncomfortable Close Encounter of the Bird Kind (and risk shooting what was very probably somebody's mother), I beat a hasty retreat over to the next dry wash. On another occasion, I had spent a fruitless twilight trying to call some coyotes within range of my .44 Dragoon. Holstering my horse pistol, I decided to call it a day and was heading back to the car, when I remembered I had left a tin of caps on the rock I had been leaning against. Walking back over the trail I had just traveled, I was surprised to see, in the half-glow of the desert starlight, a fresh set of coyote prints on top of my own footprints. A nervy coyote, still undetected, had been stalking *me*! Consequently, whether the game is large or small, it is always an extra measure of reassurance to have a black powder back-up man—a good friend whom you can trust. You will continue to remain friends if, before the hunt, you both decide who is going to have first shot. A flip of the coin is usually the best way to decide things. If I am the only one to bag any game during the hunt, it has always been my custom to offer my hunting partner half of the meat. It is also a code of the woods that the first hunter to draw blood, even if his shot doesn't drop the animal, has first option on claiming the head or rack if it is to be mounted.

The "backup buddy" system pays off for today's muzzleloading hunters just as it did for their counterparts 150 years ago. Here I take aim while my hunting partner, Henry "Pop" Fafara, stands poised for a follow-up shot. Note that his trigger finger is *off* the trigger until actual time of firing. This helps prevent accidental discharge when using double-set triggers.

In Chapter Five we discussed how and where to shoot. Now it's time to discuss what the muzzleloading hunter should do *after* he has shot. The first thing to do after firing your front-stuffer is to *reload*. It was a cardinal rule of the old-time hunters. Don't run after your game animal to see if he has dropped because if he hasn't, you've got nothing to shoot him with. (However, you should observe the direction in which he is running.) With a single shot muzzleloader, the instant you fire you are unarmed. So get your reflexes conditioned to start pouring powder and ball immediately. Off season, you might want to practice this fire and reload procedure so that it becomes second nature. Using a Mini-Ball and pre-measured charges, you should be able to get your time down to thirty seconds, and slightly longer for a patched ball. Just do not omit any of the important steps, such as pouring the powder *first* and ramming the ball *all the way home*. With your rifle charged and primed, you are now ready to follow the blood trail (and with a .50 or larger hole, there *will* be one).

Assuming your quarry has been hit, you will observe him in one of three conditions: (1) he will be dead; (2) he will be found wounded, whereby you take careful aim and dispatch him as quickly and cleanly as possible; or (3) he will be seen running. In this situation, you should try for another carefully-placed shot to bring him down, or you must trail him until you can locate and dispatch him.

Approach all downed game with caution; watch for any signs of movement, especially around the eyes. Take no chances. Advance towards any fallen big game animal from the back side, away from his feet, horns and head. Carry your rifle loaded and cocked, holding it in your shooting hand, ready to fire. Prod the carcass with a long stick or your ramrod, not with your rifle; otherwise, if the animal should be alive and suddenly springs to its feet, the action could knock your rifle aside and cause it to fire wildly. When in doubt, place a finishing shot into the heart, brain or spine.

You should always locate and bring your dead game home; never leave it because it is in some inaccessible spot. I once reluctantly passed up a shot at a six-point buck because he was standing rib-deep in a briar patch that was at the bottom of a 50-foot canyon and there was no way I could have gotten that magnificently antlered creature out.

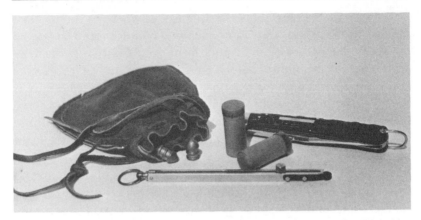

Basic items for hunting with a caplock can all be carried in one pocket if need be: pouch with bullets, pre-measured powder charges, and straightline capper. Pocket knife is used for small game; for big game, a hunting/skinning knife is carried on belt. Flintlock shooters need only add container for priming powder.

It is obvious by now that because of the weapon he chooses and the extra demands he places upon himself, there are times when the muzzleloading hunter must pass up a shot that he might otherwise have taken. That is part of the challenge of the sport. However, there are other challenges that are not as self-imposed, and bring out the fact that hunting with a front-loader really is a natural method of harvesting game. For example, unlike the metallic cartridge hunter who uses a light-gathering scope to stretch his hunting time, the muzzleloading hunter, by virtue of his open sights, cuts his twilight hunting activities short by approximately a half-hour. When it is too dark to see, it is too dark to shoot. (Besides, most states have rules prohibiting big game hunting after sundown.) That means the black powder sportsman will often find himself heading back to camp well after dark. Occasionally, having not planned to stay out so long or being further from camp than he thought, he may find himself performing this feat without the aid of a flashlight. Therefore, it is important that he preserve his night vision in order to keep from wandering off the trail. It is surprising how much can be seen using just starlight and moonlight. The only exception to this is in thick forest, where it becomes totally black and, whether your eyes are open or closed, it makes no difference. If mounted on a

[222]

horse who knows the way back to camp, give him his lead (but keep a wary rein on the grass-eater who may wander off the trail, possibly dragging your unsuspecting head across a low-lying tree limb). If you do have a flashlight, remember, a single brief beam of light can destroy a horse's night vision (and your own) for ten to thirty minutes. If you are traveling on foot by starlight and find you must use your flashlight briefly, close one eye; you'll lose your depth perception but will retain 50 percent of your night vision. In dim light, you will find that you can actually see better by not looking directly at an object; your peripheral vision has better light-gathering abilities than the center of the eye.

Because his gun, game, and equipment are so susceptible to the weather, the black powder sportsman should make it a point to become familiar with cloud patterns and the various methods of short-range weather forecasting. Sporty's Tool Shop and other aviation-oriented suppliers often have excellent weather maps for sale. You might also see what your local library has in the way of basic weather forecasting books so that you can offer more than just a guess as to whether or not your next black powder hunt will be wet or dry.

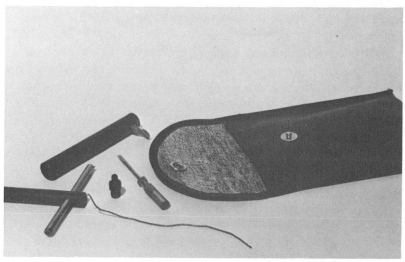

Every hunter should carry a "trouble kit" with him into the field. My pocket-sized pouch includes nipple wrench, extra nipple, small screwdriver, powder measure, and wire for nipple or vent pick.

Just as inclement weather can be a hindrance for the muzzle-loading hunter, it can also be his friend. A wet or moist forest floor can help silence your footsteps. High humidity in the air will create soft black powder fouling, making reloading for your second shot faster and easier. In addition, most wildlife can sense the approach of bad weather, and activity will be greater during the days just preceding a storm front, as game starts gathering additional food or begins moving out of the area. These "prelude days" are ideal times in which to hunt. Just be sure you carry adequate food and shelter with you into the field, should you get caught in the approaching storm, which can instantly transform itself from the hunter's friend to one of his deadliest enemies. If you have access to a shortwave or portable radio, stay tuned to the latest weathercasts. Always inform your family and local authorities of which area you plan to hunt.

The muzzleloading sportsman, by his very nature, is destined to be just a bit more particular about his hunting habits than his fellow outdoorsman, so make it a point to hunt as far away from them as possible. That means away from the roads, slamming car doors, trail bikes and audible conversations of other men. Immerse yourself in the quiet of the forest. In some overcrowded hunting areas this may be difficult, but the farther you are from other people and the sounds of civilization, the better your chances of spotting big game.

Black powder hunting is not a hurried sport. It is a time to move slowly, cautiously, yet with every sense tuned to a razor-sharp edge of alertness. When stalking, plan on covering very little ground during the day. You will take two steps, and listen for the time it takes to step off five more slow paces. If you get fatigued, sit down and rest, but keep your rifle at the ready. Game animals rarely give preliminary warning of their presence; they just seem to appear.

In hunting with a muzzleloader, the still hunter has the advantage, for he makes the animal come to *him*. For this to happen, you must remain hidden and motionless for long periods of time, some-times as much as five hours. A good, concealable blind can be the difference in your hunting success, especially if you take the time beforehand to make yourself as comfortable as possible. You will be less likely to move and fidget if you are uncramped. For afternoon hunters, try to position your blind so that you are facing east. This will put the sun at your back and will cast a few extra minutes of light over your hunting area at sundown. A blanket or piece of heavy cloth on the ground can keep the earth's chill from seeping into your bones. If there is a tree or rock to lean against, place a blanket behind your back to act as a cushion. Be sure to cut away any overhanging branches and thick brush that may obscure your field of vision. If it looks like a thunderstorm is building up, place your poncho over you before you settle in your blind, in order to avoid unnecessary movements when the rain starts falling; that could be just the time a buck may cross in front of you as he heads out for sheltered ground. Sometimes you can be just as easily concealed by sitting in *front* of thick, bushy areas, as long as you blend in with your background and do not make any sudden movements. Finally, if you feel a sneeze coming on, you can maintain your sylvan silence by placing

By finding a concealed spot downwind from well-used game trail or feeding area, the black powder still hunter usually has time to place a well-aimed shot. Note the second rifle I keep handy for a fast follow-up shot, a technique I often use for dangerous game.

a finger between your nose and your lip (where your moustache would be) and pressing. This will temporarily stop the blood flow to the nerves in your nostrils; the "tickle" will go away, and the sneeze will be averted, enabling you to maintain your vigil without a sound.

But movement and unnecessary noise are not the only things the muzzleloading hunter must guard against. There is also the ever-present aroma of your body odor. In the field, your own worst enemy is yourself. Therefore it is important to keep your man-scent a secret. Most animals find it repulsive and it is a clear danger signal

The still hunter's blind should offer a good solid rest for the rifle and an unobstructed view of the terrain. Note the presence of ready-to-go Quick Loader in case a fast follow-up shot is needed.

[226]

to them, as is any foreign odor in the wilds. Although rarely at a loss for words, I am usually rendered speechless when I see otherwise skillful hunters splashing handfuls of cologne on themselves before leaving base camp for a day's hunt. The same is true of underarm deodorant. These artificial smells only add to the problem of keeping your scent undetected. Use an unscented deodorant if you must use any. Personally, when I am on a hunt I wash with only soap and water. After a few days on the trail, you may not be the most popular person to be with in a phone booth, but when I am hunting I want to hunt, not win a popularity contest. There is plenty of time to shower, shave and defumigate yourself when you return to civilization. As for synthetic animal scents, I personally have never found one that worked. Nothing is going to make you smell like another animal; the best any formula can hope to do is to mask your own human scent. But even the best of the artificially scented lures have their drawbacks; I suspect the aroma of a man-sized "apple" drifting through the woods can spook a buck just as sure as stepping on a dry twig. The only proven method of keeping your odor from your quarry's nostrils is always to keep downwind. I will never forget the time a guide and I were sitting behind a log watching some bear bait (as you may have guessed, the bear never showed) when a small herd of seven elk came into the clearing. The wind was with us and they never knew we were there, even though they eventually circled around and began approaching us from the side, where they had a full view of the guide and myself. We remained perfectly motionless until they got within 10 feet; you could almost count the hair in their ears. Then the wind shifted and I never saw seven huge creatures move out so fast. Why didn't I shoot, you may ask. Simple. It was a spring bear hunt and even though I had been drawn for a tag, elk season was still four months away. Hunter's luck!

Because my home is in a state that has limited hunting opportunities and an unlimited population, I do a lot of muzzleloading hunting in other areas of the country. That means I cannot always have the advantage of pre-hunt scouting of terrain and game. Although it can be expensive, hunting with a professional guide for big game in wilderness areas that are unfamiliar to the hunter can be a rewarding experience for the muzzleloading sportsman. A good guide can also be one of the most sensible expenditures you can make, for you will not have to spend your precious hunting days scouting new and unfamiliar areas for sign of game; the guide should be as familiar with his hunting country as you are with your own backyard.

In selecting a guide, do not be afraid to ask for references and then check these references out, calling or writing to the individuals named and getting their comments on hunter success, conditions of the camp, quality of the food, and general attitude of the guide. Unfortunately, there are a few "bad apples" in every professional barrel, and they should be exposed and tossed out. Monetarily and emotionally, no one can afford to settle for second best on so important an experience as the pursuit of big game. A good guide or outfitter is proud of his hunting success and will usually be more than willing to tell you everything you want to know. In return, once you have selected the guide for your hunt, there are a few things you should tell him, as many of these professional hunters are unfamiliar with the characteristics of black powder hunting. Those who have never seen a front-loader may think you will be woefully undergunned, no matter what caliber you are carrying. Guides who have experienced the dramatic thunder and smoke of a muzzleloader are sometimes convinced that our guns are capable of killing not only whatever animal we want, but the relatives that sired him as well; all, of course, with one shot. Naturally, neither belief is true and in order for the guide to be effective, he must know the following facts: (1) the practical range in which our "old-timey" guns are capable of killing; (2) the chances of our getting off a second shot within a specific time period; (3) the phenomena of smoke from our first shot that will obscure everything from view; and (4) the fact that we will let no animal get away once it has been hit by a bullet of ours.

Going on far-from-home or out-of-state hunts poses something of a hardship for the muzzleloading hunter who must travel by plane, as it is against FAA rules to transport cans or other containers (i.e. horns) of black powder, even if it is locked in your checked-in baggage. However, it is perfectly legal to take along individually loaded, pre-measured charges, which fall into the same category as individual rounds of ammunition. The only stipulation is that these charges be locked in your baggage and checked in with the airline. J. B. Hodgdon, who with his brother Bob heads up the firm that makes Pyrodex, offers an easy solution; he just fills empty 12-gauge shotgun cases with powder and seals off the ends with another case or a plastic cap. As an alternative method, I fill Butler Creek's Quick Loaders up with my pre-measured charges and a greased Mini and pack them in with the rest of my checked-in luggage. Aside from these two methods, the only other choice you have is to buy a can of powder when you arrive for your hunt (a waste of money, for you will probably not go through an entire can unless you plan to be out for a year or more, in which case that is not a hunt, but a way of life!), or plan on borrowing some powder from a friend once you arrive at your destination.

Hunters traveling by car, train, or bus have no such problem, although your muzzleloader must be transported unloaded. That means an empty bore and no priming. While hunting, some states view a black powder gun as being unloaded if there is no charge in the pan or cap on the nipple, even though powder and ball may be seated in the bore. (That makes sense, as the gun cannot be fired.) However, a good rule to follow is never to load your muzzleloader until you are at the scene, ready to hunt. That also means de-capping your percussion or dumping out the priming charge of your flintlock before getting into a motor vehicle or onto a horse for the journey to and from your hunting area. It is a safe habit to get into and also assures that your priming will always be fresh.

When traveling on public transportation, it is always a good idea to have your black powder rifle, pistol or shotgun *locked* in a protective case. For pistols, this can be your suitcase; for long guns, Doskocil and Alco are two manufacturers I have found whose cases can withstand the battering around most airlines like to give them; of the two, Alco is the only firm making a case long enough for Kentuckies with barrels of 40 inches or more. I have used the Doskocil double rifle case for transporting not only rifles, but my back-up pistol and hunting knife as well. Remember, even though you must check in your gun case for all airline travel, you are also required to declare the fact that they are firearms to the ticket agent or baggage clerk or other designated official of the airlines. You will probably be asked to open the case for a visual inspection. I have found that most airlines' officials are not familiar with black powder rifles and view the guns with a certain amount of interest. (One airline employee in a popular Rocky Mountain hunting area, upon

[229]

seeing the two Hawkens I was checking in, promptly offered to sell me some "green" beaver skins. I passed on the deal.) I usually take a few minutes to tell them how a front-stuffer works, which also reassures them that the gun is safe and unfirable. Here's another handy hint: When shipping your rifles and shotguns, you may want to remove the ramrod and pack it alongside your gun; sometimes a sharp jolt can cause the ramrod to snap if it is secured under the barrel.

As an added precaution when transporting my black powder firearms, I always take black-and-white photographs of the guns (including close-ups of unalterable features such as wood grain of the stock) and make a note of the serial number. That way you will have an exacting description to give the authorities should you be the victim of some of society's lesser elements. The photographs can be of tremendous aid to law enforcement officials, as many modern-day police do not know the difference between a plains gun and a musket; no fault of theirs, we just happen to be living in different times. Finally, when shipping your muzzleloader, have it insured for its replacement value should it become lost or stolen.

Traveling *to* a hunt is one thing, but traveling *on* a hunt involves a different set of precautions: Much big game hunting is sandwiched in between a lot of jostling over rugged country on either horseback or four-wheel-drive vehicles. That means your loaded rifle will be taking a good many bumps before being fired. Therefore, as soon as you pull it from the scabbard or take it down from the vehicle's gun rack, give your load a couple of tamps with the ramrod, making sure the bullet is seated against the powder and has not slipped forward in the barrel during a rough ride to the hunting grounds. My compadre Slim Pickens once told me of riding all day with another fellow on a a black powder hunt and not finding any game. Upon dismounting back at camp, the other hunter withdrew his muzzleloading rifle and saw some powder trickling out of the bore. Upon reaching down to the bottom of his scabbard, he found the ball, which had gradually worked its way down the tube during the day. This was one time when not seeing any game to shoot at probably saved his life. Or at least his rifle and hand. In a double-barreled rifle or shotgun, the remaining charge should be rechecked after firing one bore, for the components in the remaining barrel could be moved forward by the recoil, creating a dangerous air gap between bullet and breech.

During a long stalk or climb, train yourself to check your rifle periodically to make sure the cap is still on the nipple or that your flint and priming charge are ready to go. I will never forget the time I was still hunting for deer near Prescott, Arizona. Nestled down behind some brush and rocks within 30 feet of a known game trail, I was alerted by some snapping and popping of brush directly below me. As I cocked my percussion rifle, I was horrified to see that the cap had stuck to the hammer and then promptly dropped off onto the ground below. By the time I recapped, the noise in the brush was gone, and so was whatever had made it. Ever since then, I always pinch in the sides of my caps slightly, to make sure they fit tightly on the nipple.

Checking on the condition of your equipment is something that should be done both before and during your hunt. However, checking on the condition of yourself must be done well in advance. The hunter who is overweight or short of breath is not the best candidate to be lugging a heavy octagon-barreled rifle over unpaved ground. As far as physical conditioning goes, I should state that I hate to jog, and I was once seriously thinking about starting a religion based upon pizzas and whipped-cream pies. But after a few hunts in which I felt my heart was about to pound right through my chest and I was huffing and puffing so hard I could not hold steady on my target, I altered my eating and exercise habits enough to bring me in tune with my chosen sport. That is not to say that we all must try out for the Olympics or enter the Mr. Muzzleloading America competition; it just means that we should make a continual effort to keep our weight under control, and should get in the habit of doing some simple daily exercises, such as sit-ups, push-ups, and leg-bends. This makes carrying and aiming a heavy mountain rifle much easier. Of course, there are many members of our front-stuffing fraternity who will want to delve much deeper into the physical conditioning aspect of our sport, and it is always a good idea to check with the family doctor before getting into any strenuous activity. But for me, twenty minutes a day keeps me in shape. I firmly believe that if I did not have my hunts to look forward to, I probably would not be exercising at all. Black powder hunting really is a healthy sport that could add years to your life.

As wholesome as muzzleloading hunting is, I also like it because it makes room for a few vices, if taken in moderation. For ex-

Loading on horseback. Note rifle butt wedged against boot in stirrup for support. Loading from pre-measured charge.

Placing patch and ball over muzzle.

Starting ball in bore with short-starter.

Ramming home the charge.

Capping.

Ho! For the hunt!

ample, when out-of-doors, I enjoy a pipe and a nip or two of my favorite bourbon. But I never indulge in either until after the hunt. The reasons are simple: only a fool would mix alcohol and gunpowder of any kind. And smoking *anything* near a black powder load is a surefire (!) way of blowing your hunting trip, often skyhigh. Back at camp, pursue life's simple pleasures, but while engaged in the hunt, take common sense along as a guide and play it safe.

Common sense can also be used to help you fill your tag. When hunting most big game animals such as deer during cold weather, carefully scout those sheltered areas you would normally seek to get warm. During the hot months of early season, pay special attention to shady areas that might pick up a little breeze, walking the west slopes of ridges during the morning and the east slopes in the afternoon. Look for well-used watering and bedding areas. Study the habits of the animals you hunt and then try to think like they would. Pre-hunt planning can be a hobby in itself and there is no such thing as having too much information or being too good a shot.

Even with all of our pre-hunt physical and mental conditioning, with the best of skills and armed with the "ultimate" black powder hunting gun, if we are successful on the hunt all will still be lost if we do not take proper care of the game we have harvested. Meat can be ruined if the animal is not gutted and cleaned immediately. This becomes especially crucial if the weather is warm, but no meat will last more than twenty-four hours in any kind of hunting climate. The game must be gutted first, and then skinned to keep the strong flavor in the hide from permeating the meat. This is what is meant by the "wild" taste of game; it doesn't occur if you clean and skin the animal promptly. (Do not confuse "gamey" taste with "unusual flavor." Remember, unlike Americans of the last century, we are not used to eating wild game, which was once common in meat markets throughout the U.S., where venison and bear hung alongside pigs, chickens and beef.)

Cleaning small game is easy and, due to their size, rather simple. Gather up a bunch of skin just under the animal's rib cage and slit it open with your knife. Cut the skin open from the slit (roughly in the middle of the underside) to the vent, being careful not to puncture any of the internal organs, which can taint the meat. Carefully pull out the fleshy diaphragm sack tucked into the rib cage, cut out the windpipe and roll the animal over. You might have to cut a few strands here and there, but everything that is loose should fall out and onto the ground. Cut through the pelvic bone and remove the droppings.

Skinning small animals can be accomplished by either careful slicing and peeling, or by a much faster method which I first learned in Arizona: cut off the head and feet. Next, make a slit in the skin along the back, near the neck, and start slicing a "flap" of skin away from the meat. As soon as you have a piece of loose skin about 3 to 4 inches long, place the flap under your boot (another reason why you don't want to wear moccasins on a hunt) and, holding the front legs of the animal, pull up sharply. By repeating this procedure, you will be able to yank off all of the hair-covered hide in a relatively short time. Your small game is now ready to be transported back to camp or home, where it should be washed as soon as possible.

Gutting and skinning big game animals is a hefty chore, and the proper procedure is crucial in order to save as much meat as you can. The steaks, chops and hamburger from big game can go a long way towards helping offset the cost of the hunt. One of the best methods of in-the-field game care comes from Browning Arms, and it is reprinted here with their permission:

Procedure for Field Dressing Big Game Animals

Turn the animal on its back, head uphill if possible, to facilitate the removal of entrails from the hind quarters. Make a deep circular incision around the rectum, and if string is handy tie a strong knot around the intestine. (This prevents intestinal fluids from escaping into body cavity.)

With your fingers, locate the V-shaped beginning of the breastbone. Carefully insert the knife and cut toward the hind quarters. The direction of this cut is with the lay of the hair, which minimizes cutting the hair and getting it on the meat. With two fingers of the opposite hand, hold the abdominal skin high and guide the knife blade so it doesn't cut into the intestines (which should be avoided at all costs). When the genital organs are reached, encircle them widely, and with string tie them off so no excretory fluids escape. Continue the cut to the rectum. It is not necessary to split the pelvic bone, but you may wish to do so to facilitate removing the large intestine.

Again, commencing just below the rib cage, enter the body cavity and cut through the diaphragm (tissue that separates heart and lungs from abdomen). Reach into the upper neck and cut the esophagus and windpipe free. Now carefully remove the heart and liver and save in a fabric sack, if you wish to cook these delicacies later. Gently remove the entrails, cutting any connecting tissues that offer resistance as you move through the body cavity.

Throughly drain all blood from the body cavity. You may have to turn the animal over and prop open the body cavity to do this.

The animal should be cooled as quickly as possible. In camp hang the animal from a tree in a well-ventilated area and prop the cavity open with sticks. Wash the cavity with water (salt water is excellent). Keep out dirt and insects.

Cooling can be hastened by skinning the animal as soon as practical after field dressing. The hair of deer and many other big game animals is hollow and affords excellent insulating properties keeping the animal warm. However, on a deer-sized animal, cooling from the body cavity is usually rapid enough, and the difficulty of keeping the meat clean once the hide is removed can be a problem.

If you wish to have the head mounted, make a cut just behind the shoulders. Peel off the hide to the base of the skull and cut off the head at that point. Liberally salt the flesh side of the hide and roll up the neck skin with fur outside. Store in a cardboard box in a cool, dry place and take to the taxidermist as soon as possible.

Even with our advance planning and knowledge, when that moment of truth comes at last and your black powder gun roars through the stilled air and your trophy is down, it seems that the pull of the trigger has been all too fleeting. Indeed, some of the best moments of my hunts are in my memory, where they can be relived again and again. Thus, the pride of the hunt becomes a part of our life. Some of these precious moments can be shared with others, not the least of which is the presentation of the hunter's skill at the dinner table. Therefore, I offer the next chapter as a fitting salute to your success as a muzzleloading hunter.

CHAPTER NINE

MUZZLELOADING MEALS

I f, as the old axiom goes, "Shootin' th' critter is the easiest part of huntin'," and gutting, skinning, and packing the animal out are the hardest, then eating the succulent result of a successful hunt surely must be the most internally rewarding. In the sincere hope that during your muzzleloading hunting career you will have a chance to taste all of them, my wife and I take culinary pleasure in offering you ten of our favorite wild game recipes. *Bon appetit* — which means, let's chow down!

ONE-SHOT VENISON STEW

Between the whitetail, blacktail, and mule deer, these cautious and beautifully graceful animals cover the entire country. No wonder they are our most popular big game animal. I guess that's why venison recipes are in such abundance. This recipe, while not the fanciest, is one of my favorites. It seems to be especially palatable on a cold December evening, especially if there is a storm brewing outside. It is interesting to note that it takes a buck two to four hours to eat his fill, but with this stew, I can do it in less than half an hour.

2 lbs. venison, cut into 1-inch cubes	1 tsp. paprika
3 tbsps. butter	½ tsp. marjoram leaves
¼ cup flour	⅛ tsp. tarragon leaves
1 tsp. salt	3 sprigs fresh parsley, minced
¼ tsp. freshly ground pepper	½ cup beef bouillon
2 onions, quartered	½ cup rhine wine
1 bay leaf	1 bunch carrots, cut into 2-inch pieces
	4 turnips, quartered

Dust venison with a mixture of the flour, salt, and pepper. Melt butter in a stewpot and brown the venison. Add onions, seasonings, bouillon, and wine. Cover and simmer 1½ to 2 hours. Taste and adjust seasonings. Add vegetables and continue cooking until tender, about 30 minutes. Serves four.

ROCKY MOUNTAIN ELK STROGANOFF

A magnificent animal deserves a magnificent recipe, and this is it! By far the tastiest of game animals, the elk's keen sense of smell is exemplified in the aroma that will fill your kitchen when preparing this dish. The best time to hunt elk is in early autumn, during the rut, but anytime is right for Rocky Mountain Elk Stroganoff. If you like wine, this dish warrants the purchase of a special bottle of 1973 Cabernet Sauvignon from one of the better California vintners.

4 elk sirloin steaks, cut
    into ½-inch strips
2 tbsps. minced onion
1 tsp. paprika
¼ tsp. salt

Dash nutmeg
¼ lb. fresh mushrooms,
    sliced
1 shot glass of dry sherry
¾ cup of sour cream, at
    room temperature

Brown elk in butter. Add onion, paprika, salt, nutmeg, mushrooms, and sherry. Cover and simmer until tender, about 30 minutes. Very *slowly* stir sour cream into elk mixture. Continue cooking for a few minutes. Serve over rice or noodles. Serves four.

BLACK BEAR CORN-FRIED STEAK

I've only eaten this dish once, and as you might have guessed from reading the preceding chapter, the bear that supplied the steaks wasn't mine. But someday the Hacker Bear will find his way into my buckhorn sights. In the meantime, should you be luckier than I, this recipe does a lot to glorify bear meat, which, as one game processor told me, "eating it is not something you'd want to make a habit of." I should mention that all bear meat must be cooked until it is well done, as it is subject to trichinosis, just like pork.

4 bear steaks, all fat
    removed
1 cup corn meal

1 egg, beaten
2 tbsps. milk
Salt and pepper to taste

Marinade:
    ⅓ cup EACH oil, consomme, and beaujolais wine
    1 bay leaf
    6 juniper berries, crushed

Combine oil, consomme, wine, bay leaf, and juniper berries. Marinate bear steaks in this mixture *at least* overnight. Remove the bear steaks from marinade and pat dry with paper towels. Combine egg and milk. Dip the bear steaks in the egg mixture and then roll in corn meal until well coated. Brown bear steaks in hot oil. Reduce heat, cover pan and cook over low heat until tender. Extra delicious when covered with brown gravy. Serves four.

[241]

ALASKAN SHEEP CURRY

I've yet to hunt sheep where I haven't been frozen off of the mountaintops, so when my wife devised this recipe, I thought the curry would help warm things up a bit (you can get medium hot or superhot, the way some of our buckskinning friends in England like it). Not counting the sub-species, there are three basic varieties of sheep (Dall, Stone, and Bighorn) inhabiting the western and northern regions of the United States. They are one of the most strenuous game animals to hunt, primarily due to the lofty and often inaccessible terrain they inhabit. No less challenging, however, is the task of finding a decent recipe for these curled-horn trophies. They seem as elusive as the rams themselves. To unearth this one, which became necessary after I unexpectedly took my first ram a few years ago, my wife ended up searching through some old Australian cookbooks — it seems the folks "down under" have a penchant for mutton that few nations can match. However, it is a far cry from the "recipe" given to me by a successful sheep hunter from Kentucky who dropped his ram the day after I got mine. "My wife's got the best danged way of cookin' sheep you'll ever see," he told me as I was sitting on the porch of our cabin, checking over the cracked stock my sheep hunt had netted me. "She just slices up that sheep meat, throws a little salt on it and sticks it in the oven. Best sheep I've ever eaten." Well, I never have forgotten that straightforward recipe, and I appreciated the fellow's helpfulness, but I still think Joan's version is better.

2 lbs. sheep shoulder, cubed	½ tsp. paprika
3 cloves garlic, chopped	½ tsp. ground ginger
3 onions, chopped	¼ tsp. cayenne pepper, or to taste
½ cup corn oil	Dash or two of ground cardamom
1½ tsps. salt	1 tsp. sugar
2 tsps. ground coriander	1½ cups good meat stock
1½ tsps. cumin	

Heat oil in large, heavy saucepan. Brown onions and garlic. Then add coriander, cumin, paprika, ginger, cayenne pepper, and cardamom to pan. Cook for a few minutes. Add salted sheep to pan and brown. Next add stock and stir. Sprinkle sugar over top and stir all ingredients again. Cover and simmer for 1½ hours. Allow more cooking time and ½ tsp. extra salt if using mutton. When serving, pass around small bowls of chutney, peanuts, and grated fresh coconut to sprinkle on the meat. Serves four.

WILD BOAR CHOPS

"Wild" is an apt description of both the beast and his meat; I've never tasted a richer game animal — nor have I seen an uglier creature. The wild boar that supplied the steaks for this feast was heading towards me at a fast trot with his head down, and I never will forget the shot. Likewise, I will never forget the full, rich taste of this recipe. Delicious, but you may not be able to finish the platter at one sitting.

8 boar chops, ½-inch thick
¼ cup flour
¼ tsp. EACH dry mustard, salt, ground white pepper
3 tbsps. butter

¼ cup beef bouillon
¼ cup chablis
Juice of 1 small lemon
1 tbsp. fresh chopped chives
1½ tsps. Worcestershire sauce

Combine flour, dry mustard, salt, and pepper. Coat boar chops with this mixture. Brown chops in butter. Add bouillon and wine. Cover and simmer one hour. Remove chops from pan to serving platter, keep warm. Boil down pan juices to one-half. Add lemon juice, chives, and Worcestershire sauce. Bring to boil again. Taste and adjust seasonings. Pour sauce over boar chops and serve immediately. Makes four servings.

RABBIT A LA RUXTON

George Frederick Ruxton was an educated English adventurer and sportsman who visited the American Far West and the Rocky Mountains during the time the traders and trappers were still inhabiting them and living the style of life that has been so romanticized today. Because of this, and of his literary bent, Ruxton became one of the first to write accurately about the American Mountain Man. His works were widely read and well received, especially in Europe, where he became known as Ruxton of the Rockies. A member of the Royal Geographical Society and the Ethnological Society of London, Ruxton's later adventures in Ireland, Africa, and Mexico could never erase the lure of his beloved Rockies. It was while he was on his way for a second, long-awaited return trip to the Shining Mountains, as the mountain men called them, that Ruxton fell ill in St. Louis and died. He was only twenty-seven years old. A refined man of wealth who loved to hunt, it seemed only fitting to christen this rather elegant rabbit delicacy after him. In his tent, under the slope of a mountain, with perhaps a crystal decanter of wine nearby, it might be just the dish he would whip up before riding off to explore Yellowstone the next day. Rabbit *a la* Ruxton works equally well with any cottontail, but is perhaps at its esthetic best when made with the Western cottontail.

2 small rabbits cut into serving pieces	1 tbsp. minced onion
¼ cup flour	1 large stalk celery, chopped
½ tsp. salt	1 tart apple, chopped
¼ tsp. white pepper	¾ cup chenin blanc wine
¼ tsp. marjoram leaves	¼ cup chicken bouillon
3 tbsps. butter	¾ cup cream
	3 egg yolks

Soak rabbits in salted water for 2 hours. Pat rabbits dry with paper towel. Then combine flour, salt, white pepper, and marjoram in brown paper bag. Add rabbits one piece at a time to bag, and shake to coat thoroughly. Brown rabbits in butter. Place in deep casserole. Add onion, celery, apple, wine, and bouillon. Cover and simmer until tender, about 45 minutes to an hour. Remove rabbit, celery, and apple from casserole. Place on serving platter and keep warm. Beat cream and egg yolks together. *Slowly* add this mixture to casserole juices. Cook and stir just until thick. Taste and adjust seasonings, if necessary. Pour sauce over rabbit. Garnish with sprigs of watercress. Serves four.

CHESAPEAKE HONEY-ORANGE GLAZE DUCK

Years ago I saw a sunrise over Chesapeake Bay that filled the cold morning sky with the most vivid yellow-orange color I had ever seen. When Joan told me of the ingredients in her famous glaze, it seemed a natural. No matter what flyway you hunt, this dish does any duck justice. If possible, try to convince the Head Chef to make extra stuffing, as my ducks never seem to hold enough.

1 large wild duck, or	1 cup raisins
2 small ducks	1 bunch celery, chopped
3 apples, chopped	

Honey Orange Glaze:

¼ cup butter	½ tsp. dry mustard
juice of 1 orange	¼ tsp. ground ginger
⅓ cup honey	⅛ tsp. white pepper

Rub duck cavity with salt and pepper. Combine apples, raisins and celery and use as a stuffing for the duck. Melt butter in saucepan, stir in honey, orange juice, dry mustard, ginger and pepper. Pour honey orange glaze over duck. Roast duck uncovered on a rack in a slow oven (325°–350°). Allow 30 minutes per pound. Baste duck with pan drippings frequently. Serves four.

Joan Hacker preparing the ultimate complement to a good hunt. Shown here is California Pheasant Creole in one of its earliest stages.

CALIFORNIA PHEASANT CREOLE

Now, I know there are few Creoles in California; most of them are down around Louisiana. But I love their cooking. However, most of my pheasant hunting is done in California, around the farmlands of the San Joaquin Valley. So it just seems natural to combine the spices from one area with the birds from another to produce a truly unifying blend, no matter where you live. Oh yes, this recipe works just as well on pheasant that are shot in the Midwest!

2 pheasants, halved or quartered
salt and ground pepper

½ to ¾ cup olive oil
2-3 tbsps. butter

California Creole Sauce:
2 large green peppers, chopped
1 medium onion, chopped
1 (28 oz.) can peeled tomatoes, chopped, reserve liquid

2 large cloves garlic, minced
1 tsp. paprika
¼ tsp. thyme
Cayenne pepper or Tabasco to taste
2 bay leaves

For Sauce: Melt butter in 3 quart saucepan. Add green pepper, onion and garlic. Saute until limp. Add tomatoes, reserved liquid and seasonings. Simmer about 15-20 minutes. (Sauce may be thickened if desired. Mix 1 tbsp. cornstarch with a small amount of *cold* water. Slowly add to sauce, stirring constantly. Cook a few minutes more.) While sauce is simmering, prepare pheasants.

Dry the cleaned pheasants with paper towels. Rub pieces with salt and pepper and brown in olive oil in a heavy casserole or dutch oven. Remove excess olive oil from dutch oven. Add pheasants, cover with California Creole Sauce. Simmer slowly, covered, approximately 1 hour. Serves four to six.

BARBEQUED DOVE

This is the same recipe my wife used to fix when we were dating back in Phoenix, Arizona. I would come over to her house on Saturday night after hunting the dry washes and fields north of Scottsdale all morning. I would either bring her a box of candy or a bunch of dove breasts. Whenever I brought candy, she knew I had a bad day of hunting. But the dove breasts usually guaranteed a return visit the next day for a Sunday barbeque. Well, we eventually got married and moved away from the Valley of the Sun and the harsh beauty of the desert where I used to hunt is now wall-to-wall housing tracts, but this old recipe still tastes as good as ever.

8–12 dove breasts
¼ cup peanut oil
½ cup soy sauce

1 clove garlic, minced
1 bunch green onions, chopped
2 tbsps. sesame seeds, toasted

With a snow storm at their backs and a warm fire at their front, outfitter Paul Crittenden and I pause in our hunt to wait out an approaching blizzard, fortified by a hastily cooked meal. In this setting, even the simplest food becomes a banquet. This photo was taken with a self-timer. I used my rifle and ramrod to prop up camera.

Combine oil, soy sauce, garlic, onions and sesame seeds in large, non-metallic bowl. Add dove breasts. Marinate overnight, stirring occasionally. Remove doves from marinade. Broil over charcoal to desired doneness, basting with leftover marinade. Excellent when served on a bed of wild rice. Serves four.

OBION SQUIRREL

Whenever I think of squirrel hunting I think of Tennessee, and whenever I think of Tennessee I think of Obion County, and whenever I think of Obion County I think of squirrel hunting. So it was only natural that I christened this spicy dish properly. Some folks pronounce it O-BY-on and some other folks pronounce it O-bee-on, but either way, it's delicious.

2 squirrels, cut into serving pieces
⅓ cup flour
1 tsp. salt
½ tsp. freshly ground pepper
1 tbsp. Hungarian sweet paprika
½ tsp. basil leaves
¼ tsp. ginger
Dash nutmeg
½ cup corn oil
¼ cup brandy
2 tsps. Worcestershire sauce
¾ cup chicken bouillon
½ cup sour cream

Combine flour, salt, pepper, paprika, basil, ginger, and nutmeg. Dredge squirrel pieces in flour mixture. In heavy skillet brown squirrels in hot oil. Combine brandy, Worcestershire sauce and bouillon. Pour over squirrels. Cover and simmer about 1½ hours. Remove squirrels to serving platter, keeping warm. *Slowly* add sour cream to pan juices. Heat through. Taste and adjust seasonings. Pour sauce over squirrels and sprinkle with paprika. Serves four to six.

◀ ▸

CHAPTER TEN

OUTFITTERS & SUPPLIERS
PUBLICATIONS, ORGANIZATIONS &
OTHER SOURCES OF INFORMATION
FOR THE MUZZLELOADING HUNTER

OUTFITTERS & SUPPLIERS

Alco Carrying Cases
601 W. 26th St.
New York, NY 10001
These aluminum cases are best for travel. Sold through retail outlets.

Allen Arms
1107 Pen Rd.
Santa Fe, NM 87501
Formerly known as Western Arms.

Eddie Bauer
Fifth & Union
Seattle, WA 98124
Since 1920, this famous expedition outfitter has been especially
noted for its goosedown products. They have eleven retail stores but
primarily sell through mail order. Send for their free catalog.

L. L. Bean
Freeport, Maine 04033
One of the oldest and most reliable mail-order outfitters for out-
doorsmen. Their high-quality products are also some of the least
expensive and all prices are postpaid. Of special interest to the
hunter are their chamois shirts; the styling is from 1927 but the material, especially the tan color, looks like soft leather. I own a number of them for both hunting and for wearing around the house.
Their catalogs are free for the asking.

Bianchi Gunleather
100 Calle Cortez
Temecula, CA 92390
These superbly crafted belts and holsters should last a lifetime.

Blue Star Tipis
P.O. Box 2562
Missoula, MT 59801

Ed Bohlin Saddlery
931 N. Highland Ave.
Los Angeles, CA 90038
Custom silver and leatherwork for some of Hollywood's most famous personalities.

Browning
Route 1
Morgan, UT 84050
Their fine Mountain Rifle is only sold through retail dealers.

Buck Knives
P.O. Box 1267
El Cajon, CA 92022
Excellent quality blades for hunting and skinning; sold through retail stores only.

The Buffalo Robe
18555 Sherman Way
Reseda, CA 91335
Phil and Carolyn Young operate this well-known store which has hand-fashioned Colonial and fur-trade clothing for buckskinners and nimrods alike. They also do the costuming for many of Hollywood's television and motion picture pieces that are set in the black powder era. Custom work and beading are also available. Their catalog tells all.

Butler Creek Corporation
P.O. Box GG
Jackson Hole, WY 83001
One of the most scenically located, innovative firms for the black powder hunter. Their products may be ordered direct, or through your local sporting goods store.

CCI/Speer
P.O. Box 856
Lewiston, ID 83501
Makes some of the finest pre-cast lead balls in all popular calibers. Order direct or from your dealer.

C&H Traders
St. Louis
Route #1, Box 55
Old Colony Rd.
Defiance, MO 63341
All they make is hats, but as long as they keep their quality, that's all they need to make.

Tedd D. Cash
Cash Manufacturing Co.
816 S. Division St.
Waunakee, WI 53597
Fine crafted muzzleloading rifle parts and sights are available, as well as fur-trade era tobacco boxes and lanterns. Order direct.

Colt Firearms
150 Huyshope Ave.
Hartford, CT 06102
Their authentic re-issue cap and ball revolvers are sold only through authorized dealers.

Connecticut Valley Arms
Saybrook Road
Haddam, CT 06438
Muzzleloaders are sold through retail stores and some mail-order houses such as Gander Mountain and Dixie Gun Works. Other items may be ordered direct. Send for free catalog.

CVA
See Connecticut Valley Arms.

Dixie Gun Works
Gunpowder Lane
Union City, TN 38261
One of the largest—if not *the* largest—mail-order muzzleloading suppliers in the country. Their 500-plus page catalog contains thousands of black powder items, both replica and original, some of which cannot be found anywhere else.

Doskocil Manufacturing Co.
P.O. Box 1246
Arlington, TX 76010
Their sturdy, lockable gun cases can accommodate rifles with barrel lengths of up to 36 inches. Sold through certain mail-order firms and sporting goods stores.

Eagle Grips
Art Jewel Enterprises
P.O. Box 819
Berkeley, IL 60163
Excellent quality nineteenth century style one- and two-piece rosewood, ivory, and horn grips for all cap and ball revolvers. Custom work is also available. Primarily sold through retail gun stores, but you may write directly to the firm if you cannot find a dealer in your area.

Edwards Recoil Reducer
269 Herbert St.
Alton, IL 62002

Euroarms of America
14 W. Monmouth St.
Winchester, VA 22601
The shotguns, hunting rifles and revolvers listed in this book may be ordered through retail sporting goods stores or by some firms specializing in black powder mail order products.

Flex-Gun Rods Co.
P.O. Box 202
Dearborn, MI 48121
You may order through your local sporting goods store or direct from the address above.

Gander Mountain
P.O. Box 248
Wilmot, WI 53192
Strictly mail order. Send for their free catalog. A multitude of outdoor equipment for the hunter, aa well as some black powder pistols and rifles, are depicted. Good discount prices.

Gokeys
84 S. Wabasha St.
St. Paul, MN 55107
Established in 1850, this mail-order firm sells strictly high-quality merchandise for today's sportsman. Send for their catalog.

Green River Forge
P.O. Box 715
Roosevelt, UT 84066
A small firm that hand-makes their muzzleloaders and also sells patterns for Colonial and trader era clothing. You may have a long wait for their products, but historical accuracy is assured.

The Hawken Shop
3028 N. Lindbergh
St. Louis, MO 63074
Numerous high-quality rifle parts and shooters' accessories, many of them being original designs. Unless you live in St. Louis, you'll have to order through the mails, but their catalog is worth having.

Hodgdon Powder Co.
7710 W. 50 Hwy.
Shawnee Mission, KS 66202
A dedicated, family-owned company that has been around since 1946. Makers of Pyrodex, the replica black powder, plus a variety of muzzleloading lubricants and an excellent cleaner. Their superb products are sold through gun stores nation-wide.

Hoppe's
Penguin Industries
P.O. Box 97
Parkesburg, PA 19365
Black powder cleaning implements; sold through retail stores.

Hornady
Box 1848
Grand Island, NB 68801
Fine quality swaged lead balls are available in all popular calibers. Order from your local black powder dealer.

Hot Mini 24
c/o R. L. Carter Associates
P.O. Box 8070
Colorado Springs, CO 80907
Their chemical heat packs are only sold through retail dealers.

La Pelleterie de Fort de Chartres
Fort de Chartres State Historic Site
Prairie du Rocher, IL 62277
Handmade clothing and accessories for *any* muzzleloading period.
Order from their mail-order catalog or write for a quote on custom
designs and beadwork. Owned and operated by Pat and Karalee
Tearney, two extremely knowledgeable and dedicated people.

The George Lawrence Co.
306 S.W. First Ave.
Portland, OR 97204
Since 1857, this firm has been making holsters and scabbards for
black powder guns when they were all you could get. Now into its
third generation of family ownership, belts and holsters are still being made for all popular black powder revolvers. This is one of the
few firms to offer custom work, such as lacing and hand-carved initials. You may order direct or through your local gun dealer.

Lee (R.E.A.L. bullets)
Lee Precision Inc.
Hartford, WI 53027

Lyman Products Corp.
Rt. 147
Middlefield, CT 06455
Sold through retail stores and some direct mail firms. Makers of fine
quality black powder rifles and pistols as well as a complete line of
round and conical bullet moulds and related casting equipment.
Their Black Powder Handbook is "must" reading for all serious
shooters.

Marble's Arms Corp.
P.O. Box III
Gladstone, MI 49837
Retail sales only. Since 1897, this firm has been making fine sights and related shooting equipment.

Michaels of Oregon
See Uncle Mike's.

Mowrey Gun Works
Box 28
Iowa Park, TX 76367
If your dealer doesn't stock these guns, you may order direct for either kit, or ready-made.

Navy Arms Co.
689 Bergen Blvd.
Ridgefield, NJ 07657
One of the country's leading importers and manufacturers of black powder firearms and the firm that helped start the trend. Excellent quality and customer service. You may order direct or through your retail dealer.

Nomadics Tipi Makers
17671 Snow Creek Rd.
Bend, OR 97701
A dedicated company eager to please with their quality product.

Ox-Yoke Originals
130 Griffin Rd.
W. Suffield, CT 06093
Makers of the well-known Wonder Wads for revolvers, pre-oiled and dry-lubricated patches for hunters, and cleaning patches. Excellent quality. A variety of thicknesses are available for all popular calibers. You may order direct or through your dealer.

Parker Hale
See Navy Arms (exclusive U.S. distributor).

Pyrodex
See Hodgdon Powder Co.

Randall Knives
P.O. Box 1988
Orlando, FL 32802
One of the original custom knife makers in this country. These knives often fall into the collector category and are sold through a very few retail stores. Your best bet in obtaining this product is ordering direct, although you will probably have a six-month to a year wait, as your knife will be handmade to your order. Many custom options are available, so send for catalog first.

Red River Frontier Outfitters
P.O. Box 3114
Burbank, CA 91504
Truly authentic handmade holsters and belts for all popular nineteenth century replica revolvers. Special carving is available. They also make superb historically accurate clothing for the frontiersman. Shirts, gloves, hats and britches. Delivery may take up to ninety days, so order well in advance. Mail order only from their fascinating catalog.

Remington Arms Co.
Bridgeport, CT 06602
Makers of excellent quality Hot Caps. Sold only through retail sporting goods stores.

RIG Products
P.O. Box 1488
Canoga Park, CA 91304
Usually sold through a variety of retail stores. Excellent de-greaser and protective oil spray.

Ruger
See Sturm, Ruger & Co.

C. Sharps Arms Co.
P.O. Box 885
Big Timber, MT 59011
    AND
37 Potter St.
Farmingdale, NY 11735
Their excellent reproduction of the Sharps rifle may be ordered directly from either of the above addresses (whichever is nearest you), or from your local gun store. However, the custom Sharps, such as the Gemmer, should be ordered through their Big Timber address.

Shiloh Sharps
See C. Sharps Arms Co.

Sile Distributors
7 Centre Market Pl.
New York, NY 10013
Sold through retail gun stores only.

Hiram A. Smith
Whetstone Co., Inc.
1500 Sleepy Valley Rd.
Hot Springs, AR 71901
Order through your retail sporting goods dealer.

Sporty's Tool Shop
Clermont County Airport
Batavia, OH 45103
Send for their free catalog which contains a storehouse of tools, automotive, and aviation accessories as well as weather information products. Strictly mail order.

Sturm, Ruger & Co.
One Lacey Place
Southport, CT 06490
Their Old Army is available through retail gun stores and a few black powder mail order firms.

Tom Taber's Old River Place
P.O. Box 2098
Bell Gardens, CA 90201

Teton Tintypes
130 N. Cache St.
Jackson Hole, WY 83001
One of the country's last ambrotype photographers. Also does tintypes or conventional paper photography if you want to "go modern." Studio will outfit you in period clothing, although some of us dress that way normally.

Tennessee Valley Arms
P.O. Box 2022
Union City, TN 38261
Strictly mail order and one of their authentic rifles will take about six months to complete. A variety of hunting and shooting accessories are also available from their interesting catalog.

Norm Thompson
P.O. Box 3999
Portland, OR 97208
A mail order outfitter for both country and city sportsmen. Send for their catalog.

Thompson/Center Arms
Farmington Road
Rochester, NH 03867
Retail sales through sporting goods stores and some direct mail firms such as Gander Mountain.

The Tinder Box
1723 Cloverfield Blvd.
Santa Monica, CA 90404
The nation's largest chain of retail tobacco stores, this firm can supply clay pipes made from 200 year-old-molds, replica gunning boxes, and of course, more conventional hunter's needs, such as hand-blended pipe tobaccos and "cheeroot-styled" cigars. There are about 200 stores nationwide. If you cannot find one near you, write to the above address for their free catalogue.

Totally Dependable Products
P.O. Box 277
Zieglerville, PA 19492
Fine black powder cleaning products but hard to find in most stores.
Order direct.

Trail Guns Armory
1634 E. Main
League City, TX 77573
Rarely available in most gun stores, so order your rifle direct. If in
stock, delivery is usually within three weeks.

TufOil
Fluoramics, Inc.
103 Pleasant Ave.
Upper Saddle River, NJ 07458
Excellent teflon-oil for loosening up actions and protecting metal
parts. Available in many retail stores.

TVA
See Tennessee Valley Arms.

Uncle Mike's
P.O. Box 13010
Portland, OR 97213
An innovative company firmly commited to making muzzleloading
hunting a better sport than it already is. Their numerous "shooter's
aid" products are only sold through retail sporting goods stores.

Western Arms
See Allen Arms.

Winchester Sutler
Bloomery Star Rd. Box 61
Winchester, VA 22601
Makers of speed loaders and a variety of Civil War era clothing and
camping equipment for both sides. Mail order only.

BLACK POWDER PUBLICATIONS
FOR THE MUZZLELOADING HUNTER

Monthly–Black Powder

Though no magazine is devoted solely to the black powder hunter, these three publications contain shooting information of use to us all and muzzleloading hunting articles are often featured.

Muzzle Blasts
P.O. Box 67
Friendship, IN 47021
– official publication of the NMLRA

The Buckskin Report
P.O. Box 885
Big Timber, MT 59011
– official publication of the NAPR

Muzzleloader Magazine
Rt. 5, Box 347-M
Texarkana, TX 75503

Monthly–General

In addition, there are some monthly firearms magazines that include muzzleloading hunting as regular or occasional items. Listed alphabetically, the four major ones are:

The American Rifleman/The American Hunter
1600 Rhode Island Ave. N.W.
Washington, DC 20036
– official publications of the NRA.

Occasional product field tests and articles.

Guns & Ammo/Hunting Magazine
8490 Sunset Blvd.
Los Angeles, CA 90069

An informative black powder column appears in *G & A* by

noted authority Phil Spangenberger. In addition, muzzleloading field tests and hunting articles are featured throughout the year.

Guns Magazine
591 Camino de la Reina
San Diego, CA 92108

Occasional black powder articles.

Shooting Times
P.O. Box 1790
Peoria, IL 61656

Usually one article a month on new black powder firearms. Otherwise, very little product testing for the muzzleloading hunter.

Annuals

Besides the monthly magazines there are numerous annuals put out by *Guns & Ammo*, Petersen's *Hunting Magazine*, and *Gun Digest*, to name a few. All of these thick yearlies usually contain at least one article on muzzleloading hunting. Some muzzleloading firms, such as Dixie Gun Works and Navy Arms also publish a muzzleloading annual. You are advised to check your local magazine counter or sporting goods dealer for the latest offerings.

ORGANIZATIONS

Association of Importer/Manufacturers
    for Muzzleloading (AIMM)
7710 W. 63rd St.
Shawnee Mission, KS 66201

Formed in 1976, this industry association is dedicated to improving muzzleloading in terms of safety, shooter education, product quality, and legislation, and it acts as a coordinator for members in the black powder profession, including dealers and company representatives. One of their goals is to improve and standardize muzzleloading hunting regulations in this country.

Ducks Unlimited*
National Headquarters
P.O. Box 66300
Chicago, IL 60666

With each membership comes a four-color duck identification guide, which is worth the price of admission alone. You also receive six issues of their high quality magazine a year, and have the satisfaction of knowing that your dues are helping to preserve the future of our waterfowl population. Not especially a black powder organization, but one which has played a major role in the preservation of our nation's duck and geese hunting since 1937.

National Association of Primitive Mountainmen*
P.O. Box 885
Big Timber, MT 59011

Founded by John Baird in the early 1970's, this group can be called the "free trappers" of the black powder associations, and is composed of dyed-in-the-(trade) wool "buckskinners," shooters who would rather dissolve themselves in a limestone quarry in Yellowstone than be caught shooting anything but round balls or stitching their skins together with artificial sinew. Membership includes an entertaining monthly publication called *The Buckskin Report*, which, like *Muzzle Blasts*, contains ads that a black powder hunter might not otherwise see.

National Muzzle Loading Rifle Association*
Box 67
Friendship, IN 47021

Founded in 1933, the NMLRA is the black powder version of the NRA, although it does not have the political clout of the former organization. Nonetheless, its membership is composed of a number of dedicated muzzleloaders, many of whom are hunters, and good ones at that. To my mind, the primary benefit of membership is their monthly magazine, *Muzzle Blasts*, which, though more than a little "folksy" in content, contains many hidden pearls of wisdom by a few of the old-time authors, and is a virtual treasury of ads for black powder products which a hunter might never come in contact with otherwise. Well worth the membership.

[265]

National Rifle Association*
1600 Rhode Island Ave., N.W.
Washington, D.C. 20036

Founded in 1871, today the NRA is *the* vanguard of all hunters, shooters, collectors and just plain admirers of firearms. Over 2 million strong, the NRA is a major legislative force in preserving the right to keep and bear arms. Membership includes free hunter insurance, plus a yearly subscription to either the *American Rifleman* or the *American Hunter*, both excellent publications which deal in all aspects of shooting, including muzzleloading. Free hunter information service is available to all members. The NRA also sponsors black powder safety classes and has a black powder hunting awards program.

National Wildlife Federation
1412 16th St., N.W.
Washington, D.C. 20036

A conservation organization that supports hunting as a necessary means for keeping our ecosystem in balance. Membership includes a monthly subscription to their interesting nature magazine in which the photography is often as fascinating as Nature itself.

*In addition to these national organizations, almost all have local or at least regional clubs in your area. A check through the local phone book or a short note to their national headquarters might put you in touch with others in your area who share your black powder hunting enthusiasm, and could be the start of many long and mutually rewarding friendships.

FOREIGN BLACK POWDER ORGANIZATIONS

Though not necessarily hunting oriented, these organizations may be able to offer assistance to readers in the following countries desiring to pursue the sport.

AUSTRALIA
Sporting Shooters Association of Australia
P.O.B. 154
Punchbowl, N.S.W. 2196

AUSTRIA
Muzzle Loading Association Austria
Porzellangasse 13
1090 Wien

CANADA
Canadian Black Powder Federation
P.O. Box 2876 — Postal Station P
Moncton, NB, EIC 8T8

Shooting Federation of Canada
333 River Rd.
Vanier City, Ontario
KIL8B9

DENMARK
Fyenske Sortkrudt Skytter
Hunderupvej 32
5000 Odense C

FINLAND
Oriveden Ampujat Ry
PL 5
SF 35301 Orivesi

FRANCE
Federation Française de Tir
16, Avenue du Pt. Wilson
75116 Paris

GERMANY
Deutscher Schützenbund
845 Amberg
Salzstadelplatz 1

GREAT BRITAIN
The Muzzle Loaders'
Association of Great
Britain
West Hall
Higham on the Hill
Nuneaton CV13 6AN

ITALY
Archibugieri di Piemonte
Strada Ponte Verde 11/9
10131 Torino

JAPAN
National Rifle Association
of Japan
Kishi Memorial Hall,
1-1-1 Kannami
Shibuya-ku, Tokyo

NETHERLANDS
Koninklijke Nederlandse
Schutters Associatie
Bezuidenhoutseweg 205
2594 AJ 's-Gravenhage

NEW ZEALAND
New Zealand Black
Powder Federation, Inc.
32, Wellwood Terrace
Te Awanga, R.D. 2
Hastings

SOUTH AFRICA
The Historical Firearms
Society of South Africa
P.O. Box 145
Newlands, C.P. 7725

SPAIN
Federacion de Tiro Olim-
pico Espanol
Islas Cies no. 6
Madrid 35

SWEDEN
Svenska Svartskruts Skytte
Federationen
Byvägen 34
37015 Listerby

SWITZERLAND
Schweizer Vorderlader-
schützen
Stallikonerstrasse 11
8903 Birmensdorf

STATES OFFERING SPECIAL MUZZLELOADING HUNTING SEASONS

Virtually all states allow the use of muzzleloaders during regular hunting seasons. However, some states are far-sighted enough to include a separate black powder hunting season in addition to their regular dates. This creates even more interest and opportunity for the muzzleloading hunter, and in turn, brings in more revenue for businesses within those states. Hunting laws and seasons vary from area to area, and you should obtain a copy of the current hunting regulations in the state in which you plan to hunt. Most states have minimum caliber regulations (usually .36 to .40, although no big game animal such as deer, should be hunted with anything less than .50 caliber) and other rules which should be adhered to (such as use of scopes, pistols, etc.).

The Game & Fish Departments of all states are listed below. Those states offering a special black powder hunting season are marked with an asterisk (*).

* Alabama Dept. of Conservation and Natural Resources
64 N. Union St.
Montgomery, AL 36104

Alaska Board of Fish and Game
Subport Bldg.
Juneau, AK 99801

* Arizona Game and Fish Dept.
2222 W. Greenway Rd.
Phoenix, AZ 85023

* Arkansas Game and Fish Commission
Game and Fish Bldg.
Little Rock, AR 72201

* California Dept. of Fish and Game
The Resources Agency
1416 9th St.
Sacramento, CA 95814

* Colorado Dept. of Natural Resources
Division of Wildlife
6060 Broadway
Denver, CO 80216

* Connecticut Dept. of Environmental Protection
State Office Bldg.
Hartford, CT 06115

* Delaware Dept. of Natural Resources and Environmental
Control
Division of Fish and Wildlife
D Street
Dover, DE 19901

* Florida Dept. of Natural Resources
Game and Fresh Water Fish Commission
620 S. Meridian
Tallahassee, FL 32304

* Georgia State Game and Fish Division
Trinity-Washington Bldg.
270 Washington St. S.W.
Atlanta, GA 30334

Hawaii Dept. of Land and Natural Resources
Division of Fish and Game
1179 Punchbowl St.
Honolulu, HI 96813

* Idaho Fish and Game Dept.
600 S. Walnut, Box 25
Boise, ID 83707

Illinois Dept. of Conservation
State Office Bldg.
Springfield, IL 62706

Indiana Dept. of Natural Resources
Div. of Fish and Wildlife
608 State Office Bldg.
Indianapolis, IN 46204

Iowa State Conservation Commission
State Office Bldg.
300 4th St.
Des Moines, IA 50319

Kansas Forestry
Fish and Game Commission
Box 1028
Pratt, KS 67124

* Kentucky Dept. of Fish and Wildlife Resources
Capitol Plaza Tower
Frankfort, KY 40601

Louisiana Wildlife and Fisheries Commission
P.O. Box 44095, Capitol Station
Baton Rouge, LA 70804

Maine Dept. of Inland Fisheries and Game
State Office Bldg.
Augusta, ME 04330

* Maryland Fish and Wildlife Administration
Natural Resources Bldg.
Annapolis, MD 21401

* Massachusetts Div. of Fisheries and Game
100 Cambridge St.
Boston, MA 02202

* Michigan Dept. of Natural Resources
Mason Bldg.
Lansing, MI 48926

Minnesota Dept. of Natural Resources
Div. of Game and Fish
301 Centennial Bldg.
658 Cedar St.
St. Paul, MN 55101

* Mississippi Game and Fish Commission
Robert E. Lee Office Bldg.
239 N. Lamar St.
P.O. Box 451
Jackson, MS 39205

Missouri Dept. of Conservation
P.O. Box 180
Jefferson City, MO 65101

Montana Fish and Game Dept.
Helena, MT 59601

* Nebraska Game and Parks Commission
P.O. Box 30370
Lincoln, NB 68503

Nevada Dept. of Fish and Game
Box 10678
Reno, NV 89510

* New Hampshire Fish and Game Dept.
34 Bridge St.
Concord, NH 03301

New Jersey Dept. of Environmental Protection
Div. of Fish, Game, and Shellfisheries
Box 1390
Trenton, NJ 08625

* New Mexico Dept. of Game and Fish
State Capitol
Santa Fe, NM 87501

* New York Dept. of Environmental Conservation
Fish and Wildlife Division
50 Wolf Rd.
Albany, NY 12201

* North Carolina Wildlife Resources Commission
325 N. Salisbury St.
Raleigh, NC 27611

North Dakota State Game and Fish Dept.
2121 Lovett Ave.
Bismarck, ND 58501

* Ohio Dept. of Natural Resources
Division of Wildlife
Fountain Square
Columbus, OH 43224

* Oklahoma Dept. of Wildlife Conservation
P.O. Box 53465
Oklahoma City, OK 73105

* Oregon State Wildlife Commission
Box 3503
Portland, OR 97208

* Pennsylvania Game Commission
P.O. Box 1567
Harrisburg, PA 17120

Rhode Island Dept. of Natural Resources
Div. of Fish and Wildlife
83 Park St.
Providence, RI 02903

* South Carolina Wildlife Resources Dept.
Box 167
Columbia, SC 29202

* South Dakota Dept. of Game, Fish and Parks
State Office Bldg.
Pierre, SD 57501

Tennessee Game and Fish Commission
Box 40747
Ellington Agricultural Center
Nashville, TN 37220

Texas Parks and Wildlife Dept.
John H. Reagan Bldg.
Austin, TX 78701

* Utah State Dept. of Natural Resources
Division of Wildlife Resources
1596 W. N. Temple
Salt Lake City, UT 84116

Vermont Agency of Environmental Conservation
Fish and Game Dept.
Montpelier, VT 05602

* Virginia Commission of Game and Inland Fisheries
4010 W. Broad St., Box 11104
Richmond, VA 23230

* Washington Dept. of Game
600 N. Capitol Way
Olympia, WA 98504

West Virginia Dept. of Natural Resources
1800 Washington St. East
Charleston, WV 25305

* Wisconsin Dept. of Natural Resources
Division of Forestry, Wildlife and Recreation
Box 450
Madison, WI 53701

Wyoming Game and Fish Dept.
Box 1589
Cheyenne, WY 82001

INDEX

Trigger, "set," 30–31
Trouble kit for hunting, 223
TufOil, 114, 183

U

Uncle Mike's Hot Shot nipples, 177
Uncle Mike's Stalking Gun Case, 91

V

Velcro fasteners on hunting clothes,
207–210
Venison stew, 240

Vest
duck down, 203
goose down, 201–203

W

Weather forecasting in hunting,
223–224
Wild boar chops, 243
"Windage, Kentucky," 53, 155
Wounded animals, 142–143, 221

Z

Zoave Rifle, 56